5-10-15+ Fat Quarters™

Edited By Jeanne Stauffer

HOUSE of WHITE BIRCHES
PUBLISHERS
SINCE 1947

5-10-15+ Fat Quarters™

Editor **Jeanne Stauffer**
Art Director **Brad Snow**
Publishing Services Director **Brenda Gallmeyer**

Editorial Assistant **Stephanie Smith**
Assistant Art Director **Nick Pierce**
Copy Supervisor **Michelle Beck**
Copy Editors **Mary O'Donnell, Amanda Scheerer**
Technical Editor **Sandra L. Hatch**
Technical Proofreader **Angie Buckles**

Production Artist Supervisor **Erin Augsburger**
Graphic Artists **Glenda Chamberlain, Edith Teegarden**
Production Assistants **Marj Morgan, Judy Neuenschwander**
Technical Artist **Connie Rand**

Photography Supervisor **Tammy Christian**
Photography **Andrew Johnston, Matthew Owen**
Photo Stylists **Tammy Liechty, Tammy Steiner**

5-10-15+ Fat Quarters is published by DRG, 306 East Parr Road, Berne, IN 46711.
Copyright © 2010 DRG. All rights reserved. This publication may not be reproduced
in part or in whole without written permission from the publisher.

Printed in the United States of America
First printing 2010, China.
Library of Congress Control Number: 2009940641
Hardcover ISBN: 978-1-59217-298-6
Softcover ISBN: 978-1-59217-299-3

RETAIL STORES: If you would like to carry this book or any other DRG publications,
visit DRGwholesale.com

Every effort has been made to ensure that the instructions in this publication
are complete and accurate. We cannot, however, take responsibility for human
error, typographical mistakes or variations in individual work. Please visit
ClotildeCustomerCare.com to check for pattern updates.

DRGbooks.com

4 5 6 7 8 9 10

Welcome

Many people take the plunge into the hobby of quilting with the purchase of one single square of fabric—the ubiquitous fat quarter. For many there is no turning back. The fat quarter still reigns supreme as a straightforward way to purchase fabric, whether you are buying for a particular project or simply building your stash. Fabric companies have recognized the ever-present power of the fat quarter and continue to design, package and sell coordinating fabric bundles that are irresistible.

In this book, we present a variety of fun and unique projects, from small to large, designed around your love of quilting with fat quarters. We've also organized the projects in a user-friendly format, not by themes, but rather by the number of fat quarters it takes to complete a project. We think this approach makes a lot of sense—we hope you do too! Look for the fat quarter insignia to guide you in your fat quarter quilting.

4 FAT QUARTERS

Perhaps the best feature of this book is the variety of projects it contains: small decorative household items that require only a few fat quarters, to flirty purses, wall hangings and table runners, which use several more. Of course, we've included a variety of quilts, with color palettes aplenty.

From functional to fabulous—we've got you covered, 5-10-15 or more fat quarters at a time.

Happy quilting,

Jeanne Stauffer

Contents

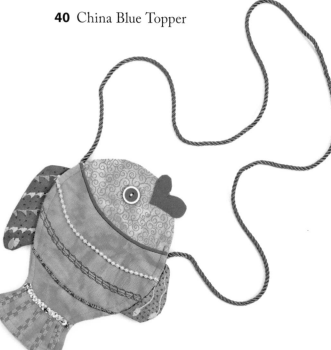

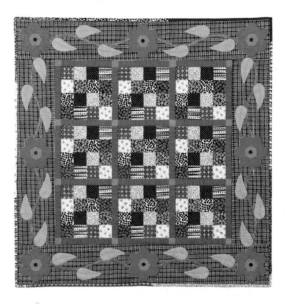

Holly Tree Skirt

Simple holly appliqués make this tree skirt extra special.

DESIGN BY CAROLYN S. VAGTS

PROJECT SPECIFICATIONS

Skill Level: Beginner
Tree Skirt Size: 36½" x 36½"

MATERIALS

- 1 fat quarter red mottled
- 1 fat quarter green mottled
- 1 yard cream tonal
- 1½ yards green print
- Fusible fleece 42" x 42"
- Backing 42" x 42"
- All-purpose thread to match fabrics
- Quilting thread
- Microtex 70/10 needle
- ½ yard 15"-wide fusible web
- Basic sewing tools and supplies

Cutting

1. Prepare templates using patterns given; cut as directed on each piece.

2. Cut eight 1½" x 18" flange strips red mottled.

3. Cut 2½"-wide bias strips to total 225" from green print for binding.

Completing the Tree Skirt

1. Trace holly leaf and berries shapes onto the paper side of the fusible web as directed on patterns for number to cut; cut out shapes, leaving a margin around each one.

2. Fuse shapes to the wrong sides of fabrics as directed on patterns for color; cut out shapes on traced lines. Remove paper backing.

3. Center and fuse two leaves and three berries 1½" from bottom edge of seven A pieces referring to Figure 1 and pattern motif for positioning of pieces.

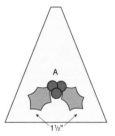

Figure 1

4. Fold each of the red mottled flange strips in half with wrong sides together along length; press.

5. Pin and stitch a flange strip to the wide end of each A piece with raw edges even as shown in Figure 2. Trim strip ends even with A.

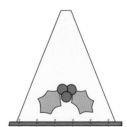

Figure 2

6. Stitch a B strip right sides together with an A/flange unit; press B to the right side. Repeat for all A/flange units. **Note:** *Flange strips may be pressed toward A or B; be consistent. They will naturally face toward A.*

7. Pin two A-B units right sides together; stitch along one long edge; press seam in one direction.

Repeat to make four A-B pairs, one pair with no appliqué motifs as shown in Figure 3.

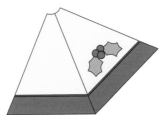

Figure 3

8. Join two A-B pairs; to make a half. Repeat to make two halves; press seams in one direction.

9. Join the two halves to make an octagon shape; press seam to one side.

10. Bond the fusible fleece to the wrong side of the octagon shape referring to manufacturer's instructions; pin-baste the backing to the fused layers.

11. Quilt as desired by hand or machine. Reduce the stitch length to 1.5–1.8 or 15–18 stitches per inch and insert a Microtex 70/10 needle. Stitch slowly, close to edges of each appliqué shape and on vein lines on leaves. ***Note:*** *If your machine has* *a needle-down selection, it will help when turning corners. If not, use the hand wheel to lower the needle before turning corners.*

12. When quilting is complete, trim excess batting and backing even with the edges of the pieced top.

13. Mark the center of the A piece without an appliqué motif; cut from the top to the bottom along the marked line to split the quilted top as shown in Figure 4.

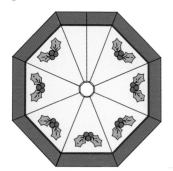

Figure 4

14. Join binding strips on short ends with diagonal seams to make one long strip as shown in Figure 5; press open.

¼"

Figure 5

15. Fold the strip in half with wrong sides together along length; press.

16. Starting at the inner circle edge of the split A-B unit, sew binding to raw edges of top side along split of A-B unit, around outer edge and back up opposite split of A-B unit to inner circle edge. Press binding to the back side; trim off leftover binding. Hand-stitch in place.

17. Press the remainder of the binding strip open and press into quarters. Fold the strip with raw edges at the center crease to make ties as shown in Figure 6.

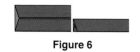

Figure 6

Place line on fold

Match on line to make complete pattern

B

A

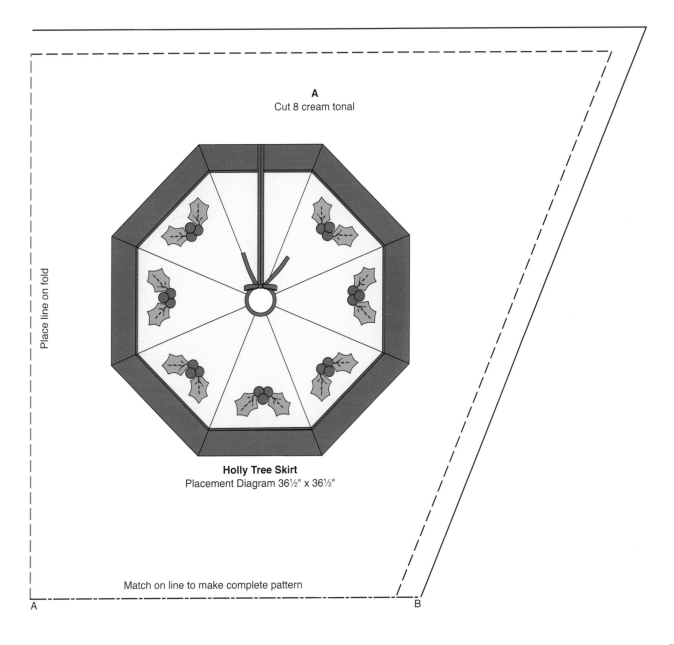

18. Find the center of the ties and pin to the center front of the inner circle and around to each side end, enclosing the raw edge of the circle inside the folded strip as shown in Figure 7.

Figure 7

19. Starting at the end of the tie, stitch up to the circle, again referring to Figure 7. Continue stitching around the circle, being careful to include both edges of the tie strip in the stitching. Continue stitching to the remaining end of the tie to complete the tree skirt. ◆

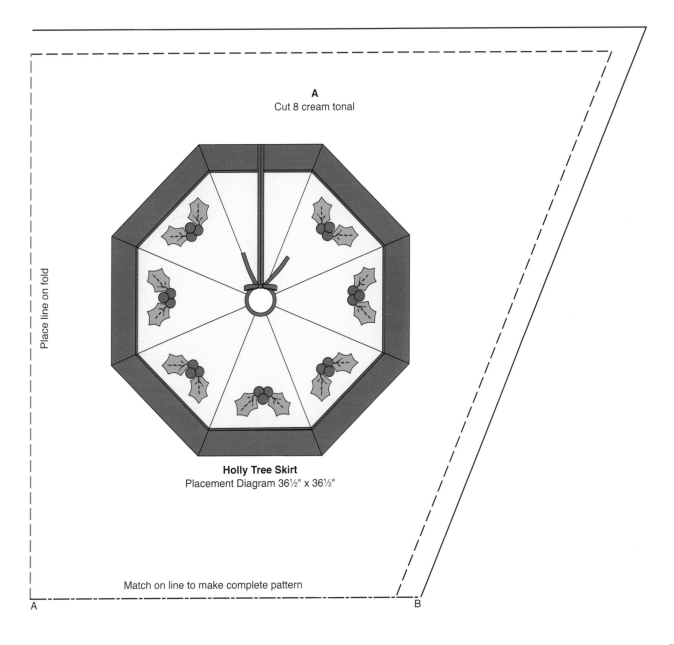

A
Cut 8 cream tonal

Place line on fold

Holly Tree Skirt
Placement Diagram 36½" x 36½"

Match on line to make complete pattern

A

B

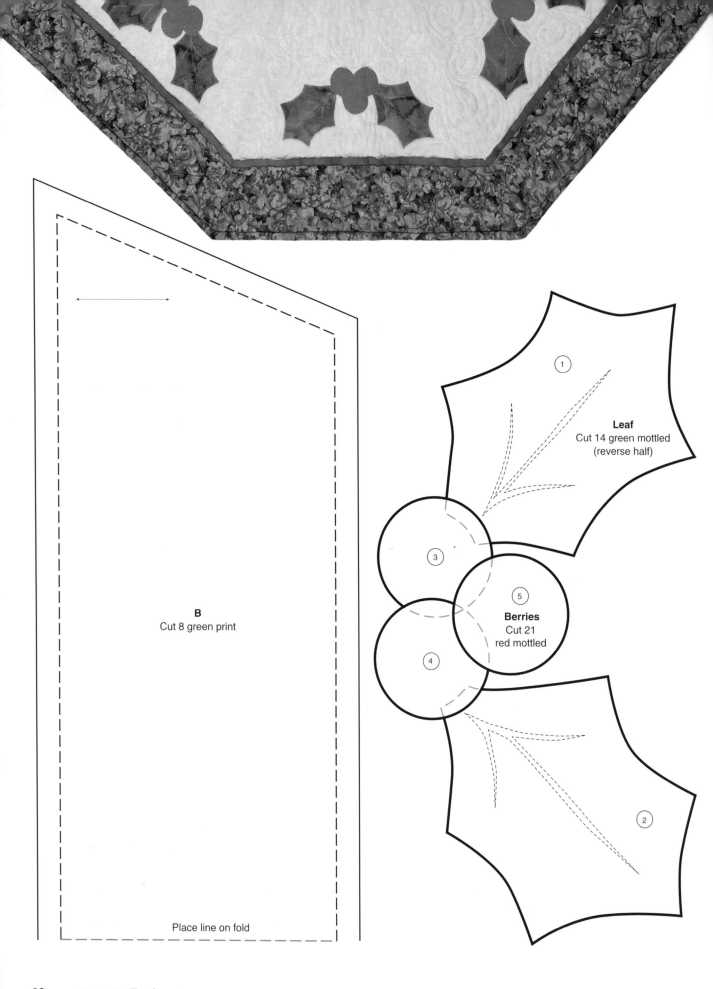

B
Cut 8 green print

Place line on fold

①
Leaf
Cut 14 green mottled
(reverse half)

③

⑤
Berries
Cut 21
red mottled

④

②

Flower-Fresh Magnet Message Board

Select fabrics to match your decor for your own magnet message board.

DESIGN BY JODI G. WARNER

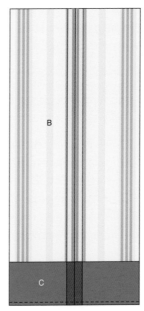

PROJECT SPECIFICATIONS

Skill Level: Beginner
Message Board Size: 9" x 20" plus hanger

MATERIALS

- 1 fat quarter pink multistripe
- 1 fat quarter chocolate tonal
- 12 (3" x 3") pink or chocolate print scraps
- All-purpose thread to match fabrics
- White all-purpose thread
- 1 (9" x 20") folded-edge metal message board with pre-drilled hanger holes
- 1 (1½") metal cover button
- .5mm mechanical pencil
- Template plastic
- Clear fabric glue
- Coordinating magnets
- Water-soluble marker
- Basic sewing tools and supplies

Cutting

1. Prepare templates using patterns given; cut as directed on A.

2. Cut one 19½" x 18" B strip pink multistripe.

3. Cut one 19½" x 3¾" C strip chocolate tonal.

4. Cut one 2½" x 21" D strip chocolate tonal for hanger.

Completing the Message Board

1. Sew C to B; press seam toward C. Press a ½" crease at the top edge of B.

2. Fold the B-C panel in half along length with right sides together; stitch center back seam. Press seam open.

3. Find the center of the lower edge; crease. Match and pin center back seam at crease. Stitch across the lower edge as shown in Figure 1.

B

C

Figure 1

4. Turn panel bag right side out; press lower edge.

5. Insert metal message board and mark pre-drilled holes onto the panel front and back with water-soluble marker for buttonhole placement; remove bag.

6. Complete ⅝" buttonholes through front and back layers separately. Clip into buttonholes; re-insert board, fold at upper crease and arrange

so board is between panel and front seam allowance; apply fabric adhesive to join the front and back seam allowances.

7. Press an A shape in half with right sides together along length; stitch across the end as shown in Figure 2, locking stitching. Trim seam allowance with a long angled cut as shown in Figure 3; press seam open.

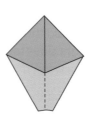

| **Figure 2** | **Figure 3** | **Figure 4** |

8. Turn right side out, pushing out point. Align center-back seam with the center-front crease as shown in Figure 4; press to complete one petal.

9. Repeat steps 7 and 8 to complete 12 petals.

10. Center stitching template on the back side of each petal; trace edges with a mechanical pencil.

11. Arrange petals in a pleasing order, then join into a ring by positioning adjacent petals right sides together and stitching on the traced lines as shown in Figure 5; press seams open. ***Note:*** *Petal seam allowance will meet at the center back; trim excess to eliminate any overlapping and reduce bulk.*

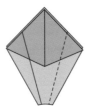

Figure 5

12. Center petal ring over board cover with ring center approximately 4" below upper edge; glue inner raw edges in place. When dry, adhere petal points in place with a dab of fabric adhesive.

13. Remove wire loop from cover button back; cut fabric circle using chocolate tonal and cover button as directed by manufacturer's instructions.

14. Center and glue the button over petal ring, hiding raw center edges as shown in Figure 6.

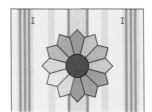

Figure 6

15. Fold the D strip with right sides together along length; stitch across each end and along long edge, leaving a 2" opening at the center as shown in Figure 7. Turn right side out through opening; press edges flat, turning in opening edges ¼".

Figure 7

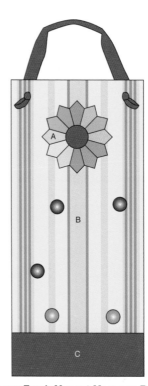

Flower-Fresh Magnet Message Board
Placement Diagram 9" x 20"

16. Fold to find the lengthwise center; mark with a pin. Fold the strip in half, bringing folded edge to stitched edge over seam opening as shown in Figure 8. ***Note:*** *This will create a narrow area to make hanging easier.*

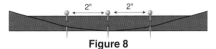

Figure 8

17. Measure and place a pin 2" on each side of the center pin, again referring to Figure 8; stitch close to edge through all layers from one pin to the other as shown in Figure 9.

Figure 9

18. Insert each end of strip from back to front through buttonholes on cover and board; tie an overhand knot with a ¾" tail.

19. Attach magnets to use as a message board. ◆

Align on fold

Stitching Template

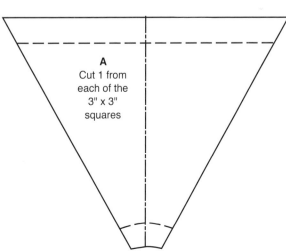

A
Cut 1 from each of the 3" x 3" squares

Stemware Coasters

Make pocket-style coasters for your stemware
and pitcher, decanter or wine bottle.

DESIGN BY NANCY RICHOUX

PROJECT NOTE

These coasters may be made with or without a
layer of flannel or thin batting between the layers
for extra absorbency.

PROJECT SPECIFICATIONS

Skill Level: Intermediate
Coaster Sizes: 4" and 7" diameters

MATERIALS

4 Pocket-Style Coasters—any size up to
  5" diameter
• 1 fat quarter fabric 1
• 1 fat quarter contrasting fabric 2

4 Prairie-Point Style Coasters
• 1 fat quarter fabric 1 (for coasters larger than
  4" diameter, a second fat quarter is needed)
• 1 fat quarter contrasting fabric 2

1 Large Coaster
• 1 fat quarter fabric 1
• 1 fat quarter contrasting fabric 2

For All Sizes
• ¼ yard flannel or thin batting (optional)
• All-purpose thread to match fabrics
• Basic sewing tools and supplies

Pocket-Style Coasters

Cutting

*Note: The size of the coaster can be changed to
accommodate stemware with different-size feet. A
variety of sizes of circle templates have been provided.*

1. Choose a circle that is 1" larger than the
diameter of the foot of your stemware; prepare a
template without seam allowance.

2. To make four small pocket-style coasters, trace
12 circles on the wrong side of fabric 1 for tops
and backings; cut out.

3. To make one large pocket-style coaster, trace
three circles in the chosen size on the wrong side
of fabric 1 for top and backing; cut out.

4. Cut enough 1"-wide
bias strips from fabric 2
to create four 18" lengths
of bias for binding for
small coaster or 27"
of bias for binding for
large coaster referring to
Figure 1.

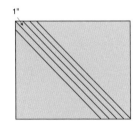

Figure 1

5. Cut four small lining circles from remainder of
fabric 2 for small coasters or one large lining circle
for large coaster.

6. Cut four small circles or one large circle from
flannel or thin batting if desired.

Completing Pocket-Style Coasters

1. Fold eight fabric 1 small circles in half with
wrong sides together matching curved edges as
shown in Figure 2; press.

Figure 2

2. For one small coaster, layer and pin as follows: fabric 1 circle wrong side up, optional flannel/thin batting circle, fabric 2 circle right side up and two folded circles with folds meeting in the center and curved edges aligned as shown in Figure 3.

Figure 3

3. Machine-baste ⅛" all around to hold layers together.

4. Press one long edge of an 18" bias strip ¼" to the wrong side.

5. Matching raw edges, pin and stitch binding around edge of the basted coaster on the folded circle side, overlapping at the beginning and end.

6. Turn the binding to the back side; hand-stitch in place to finish.

7. Repeat steps 2–6 to complete a total of four small pocket-style coasters.

8. Repeat steps 1–6 to complete one large coaster, folding two fabric 1 circles and using the 27" bias binding strip for finishing.

Prairie-Point-Style Coasters

Cutting

1. Choose a circle that is 1" larger than the diameter of the foot of your stemware; prepare a template without seam allowance.

2. To make four small prairie-point-style coasters, trace 20 circles on the wrong side of fabric 1 for tops and backings; cut out.

3. Cut enough 1"-wide bias strips from fabric 2 to create four 18" length strips of bias for binding small coaster.

4. Cut four lining circles from remainder of fabric 2.

5. Cut four circles from flannel or thin batting if desired.

Completing the Prairie-Point Style Coasters

1. Fold 16 fabric 1 circles into quarter circles as shown in Figure 4.

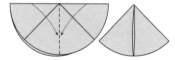

Figure 4

2. For one coaster, layer and pin as follows: fabric 1 circle wrong side up, optional flannel/thin batting

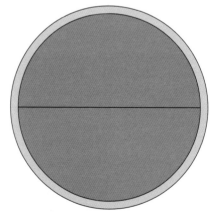

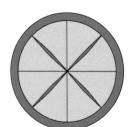

Small Prairie-Point-Style Coaster
Placement Diagram 4" diameter

Small Pocket-Style Coaster
Placement Diagram 4" diameter

Large Pocket-Style Coaster
Placement Diagram 7" diameter

circle, fabric 2 circle right side up and four folded circles with open folds right side up and meeting in the center with curved edges aligned as shown in Figure 5.

Figure 5

3. Machine-baste ⅛" all around to hold layers together.

4. Press ¼" one long edge of an 18" bias strip to the wrong side.

5. Matching raw edges, pin and stitch binding around edges of the basted coaster on the prairie-point side, overlapping at the beginning and end.

6. Turn the binding to the back side; hand-stitch in place to finish.

7. Repeat steps 2–6 to complete a total of four small prairie-point-style coasters. ◆

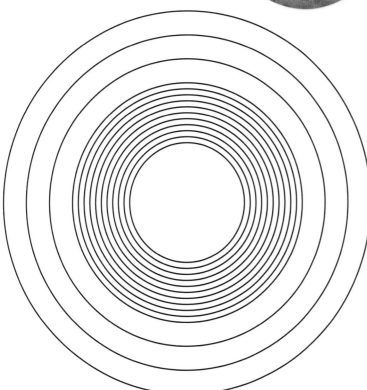

Circle Template Sizes
Enlarge 200%
2½", 2¾", 3", 3¼", 3½", 3¾", 4",
4¼", 4½", 4¾", 5", 6", 7" & 8"

Whimsical Doorstop

Keep your sewing-room door open with this multicolored quilter's doorstop.

DESIGN BY JODI G. WARNER

. . . .

PROJECT SPECIFICATIONS

Skill Level: Advanced
Doorstop Size: Approximately 9½" tall x 5½" wide

MATERIALS

- 1 fat quarter lime green mottled
- 1 fat quarter purple dot
- Scraps brown dot, turquoise multiplaid, deep green dot, yellow print, bright pink mottled, bright orchid dot and gold print
- All-purpose thread to match fabrics
- 1 empty, new quart tin can approximately 5" tall x 4¼" diameter (available at home-improvement stores)
- ⅝ yard narrow poly cord for piping
- ⅛ yard lightweight fusible web
- 1¾" length of 1⅞" diameter cardboard tube or PVC pipe
- 1½ yards yellow cord
- ⅝ yard bright pink medium-width rickrack
- 2⅝" diameter wooden beads, painted purple
- Clear acrylic quick-drying adhesive
- Template material
- 1–2 cups dry beans, rice or other material for weight
- Clear nail polish or fray preventative
- Basic sewing tools and supplies

Cutting

1. Cut one 4½" x 14¼" A rectangle lime green mottled.

2. Cut one 4¼" x 14¼" B rectangle scrap brown dot.

3. Cut one 8" x 22" C strip purple dot.

4. Cut one 4¼" x 22" D strip turquoise multiplaid.

5. Cut one 4¼" x 22" E strip and one 4½"-diameter G circle deep green dot.

6. Cut one 1" x 22" F strip yellow print for piping.

7. Cut two 2" x 21" H strips bright pink mottled.

8. Cut two 2" x 21" I strips orchid dots.

9. Trace appliqué shapes onto the paper side of the fusible web as directed on pattern for number to cut; cut out shapes, leaving a margin around each one.

10. Fuse shapes to the wrong side of fabrics as directed on each piece for color; cut out shapes on traced lines. Remove paper backing.

Instructions

1. Prepare templates for can base and handle tie end using patterns given.

2. Fold the B strip in half across the width; place the can base template on the fold, mark points and cut out.

3. Place the handle tie end template on the end of each H and I strip, mark and trim along marked lines.

4. Sew B to A along the long edge; press seam open.

5. Transfer crease lines to A in two places as shown on can base template for positioning appliqué motifs.

6. Arrange one flower motif on each crease line in numerical order with lower edge of stem on seam; fuse in place.

7. Using thread to match fabrics and a narrow zigzag stitch, stitch around each shape.

8. Center rickrack over seam between A and B as shown in Figure 1; straight-stitch in place with matching thread.

Figure 1

9. Join the first two sawtooth edges at each end of the A-B unit as shown in Figure 2; press seams to one side.

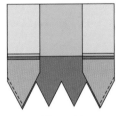 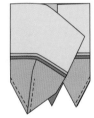

Figure 2   **Figure 3**

10. Join adjacent sawtooth edges to the previously stitched pairs so the points are joined in two three-part halves as shown in Figure 3. Repeat to join the two three-part halves.

11. Align remaining raw edges and stitch from the bottom center to outside edge of A to finish the bottom of the holder as shown in Figure 4; press as much as possible.

Figure 4

12. Fold C in half wrong sides together across width; stitch ends to form a tube; press seam open. Turn right side out; fold in half to align raw edges. Sew a line of gathering stitches ¼", 1¼" and 1¾" from edge as shown in Figure 5.

Figure 5

13. Fold and crease the body piece to mark the center opposite the seam; repeat with the C tube.

14. Pin the C ruffle to the top edge of the A-B body, matching raw edges and aligning seams and centers. Pull up the ¼" gathering threads and adjust ruffle to fit the A-B body piece; pin all around and stitch with a ¼" seam following the gathering-stitch line.

15. Prepare piping by enclosing the poly cord against the wrong side of F as shown in Figure 6; trim excess seam allowance to ¼", again referring to Figure 6.

¼"

Figure 6

16. Baste piping to the upper edge of D; join D and E right sides together, stitching on piping basting.

17. Turn right side out with D and E back to back and press. Unfold and align raw ends, matching piping seam to piping seam at ends. Stitch with a ¼" seam allowance; press seam open, then refold into a tube at piping edge. Gather-stitch ¼" and 1½" in from edge.

18. Layer an H strip with an I strip right sides together; stitch along both side edges and at the shaped end. Trim seam allowance in half and trim off point. Turn right side out; press edges flat. Repeat for second H and I strips to make two ties.

19. Align straight ends of ties and stitch with ¼" seam allowance; press seam open.

20. Place weighting material inside can and secure lid.

21. Center and securely glue the cardboard or PVC tube onto the can lid.

22. Gather-stitch edge of G; place over the tube end, pull thread to gather, tie off thread and glue lower edge in place.

23. Place raw-edge end of D-E inner ruffle tube around the base of the covered cardboard tube and pull up both rows of gathers to fit. Tie off and glue where fabrics touch.

24. Position handle ties with end seam at can bottom center; bring handles up can sides at equal distances and glue. Tie ends in neat square knot above inner ruffle.

25. Insert can assembly into body; pull up remaining gather stitching on C ruffle to fit snuggly around the inner ruffle and tube and tie off.

26. Glue the inner gathered area to adjacent surfaces.

27. Wrap cord around cinched area four times and tie a neat bow, securing with glue, if necessary.

28. Insert cord ends into beads, tie off and trim excess cord. Finish cord ends with clear nail polish or fray preventative as necessary. ◆

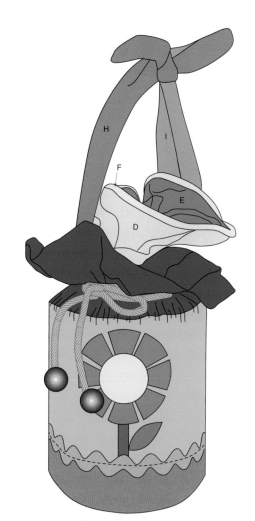

Whimsical Doorstop
Placement Diagram Approximately 9½" tall x 5½" wide

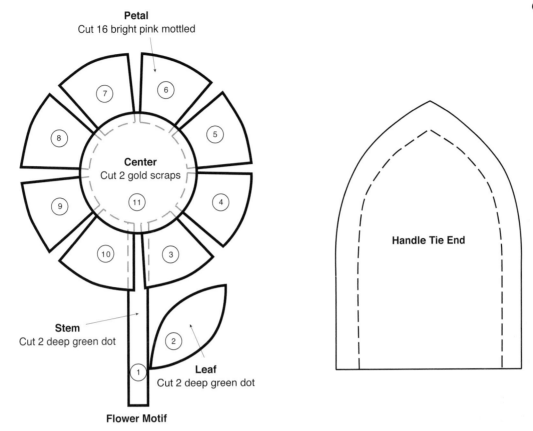

Petal
Cut 16 bright pink mottled

Center
Cut 2 gold scraps

Stem
Cut 2 deep green dot

Leaf
Cut 2 deep green dot

Flower Motif

Handle Tie End

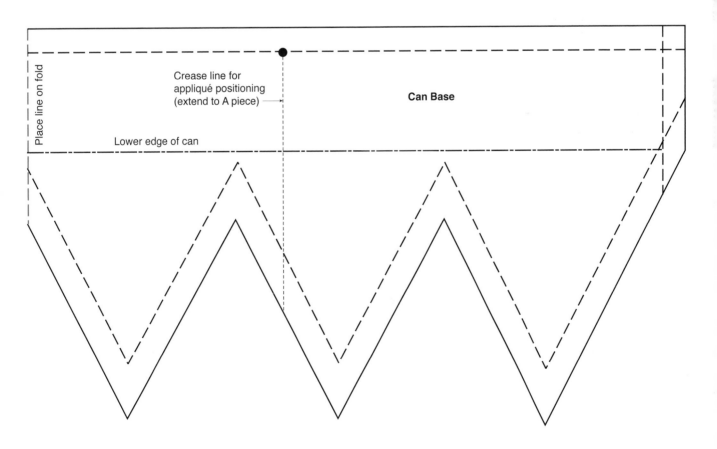

Place line on fold

Crease line for
appliqué positioning
(extend to A piece) →

Lower edge of can

Can Base

Flower Power Eyeglasses Case

Store your glasses in this bright pouch, and you'll never have to search for them again.

DESIGN BY CHRIS MALONE

PROJECT SPECIFICATIONS

Skill Level: Beginner
Case Size: 7" x 4"

MATERIALS

- 1 fat quarter multicolored floral
- 1 fat quarter coordinating green tonal
- Batting 7" x 9½"
- All-purpose thread to match fabrics
- Quilting threads to match fabrics
- Assorted colors of glass E beads
- Size 3 snap set
- Basic sewing tools and supplies

Cutting

1. Cut one 7" x 9½" rectangle each multicolored floral and green tonal.

2. Cut one 1⅛" x 20" bias strip from green tonal for binding.

Completing the Eyeglasses Case

1. Lay the floral rectangle right side up on the batting, matching the edges; round the corners on one end using the pattern given. Baste layers together all around and from corner to corner as shown in Figure 1.

Figure 1

2. Using assorted colors of quilting thread, select and hand-quilt around flowers in the print, selecting flowers from the whole area. **Note:** *Do not quilt every flower; just be sure that each area is covered. You may use fancy embroidery stitches if desired. The leaves on the sample print have been embellished with a fern stitch as shown in Figure 2.*

Figure 2

3. Add beads to some of the flower centers, using two stitches when adding a bead. Knot the thread after adding beads; do not place any beads within ½" of the raw edges.

4. Remove basting stitches when quilting is complete.

5. Place the lining right sides together with the quilted piece; stitch a ¼" seam on the straight 7" side as shown in Figure 3.

Figure 3

6. Trim batting close to seam and flip the lining over so batting is between the two fabric layers; press seam flat.

7. Hand-baste around the raw edges through all layers. If you need to press, place the piece right

side down on a thick towel and iron on the lining side.

8. Fold up the bottom straight edge 3"; machine-baste the raw edges together with a ³⁄₁₆" seam as shown in Figure 4.

9. Carefully press a ¼" hem along one raw edge of the green bias strip; fold in a ¼" hem at one end.

10. Stitch the binding strip to the outside edge of the case with raw edges even starting at a bottom corner with the hemmed end as shown in Figure 5.

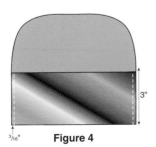

3"

³⁄₁₆"

Figure 4

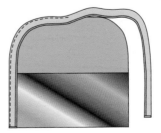

Figure 5

11. Sew all around to the other bottom corner with a ¼" seam allowance, being careful not to stretch the bias around the curves. Near the end, trim the excess binding and fold in a ¼" hem; finish the seam.

12. Fold the binding over to the other side; hand-stitch the folded edge of the binding over the previous stitching with small, invisible stitches. ***Note:*** *If the seam is too bulky, trim it slightly before folding over the bias.* Slipstitch the folded edges together at the bottom corners.

13. Fold the top of the case down about 2¼". Position a snap set under the flap and sew the halves in place. To finish, stitch through the lining and batting only on the top snap piece so the stitches do not show on the front. ◆

Flower Power Eyeglasses Case
Placement Diagram 7" x 4"

Rounded Corners Pattern

Reversible Walker Bag

These practical bags are the perfect accessory for use with a walker.

DESIGN BY LUCY A. FAZELY & MICHAEL L. BURNS

PROJECT NOTES

If making the bag for a charity, it is recommended to make two different-size pockets so the recipient has a choice. If the recipient is known, the pockets may be tailored to meet their needs.

PROJECT SPECIFICATIONS

Skill Level: Beginner
Bag Size: 17½" x 19½"

MATERIALS

- 3 coordinating fat quarters
- 2 (36") colored shoelaces
- All-purpose thread to match fabrics
- Water-soluble marker
- Basic sewing tools and supplies

Cutting

1. Set aside one fat quarter to use as the pockets; trim the remaining two fat quarters to 18" x 20".

2. Cut two 9" x 18" pieces from the pocket fabric. *Note: Pockets can be shorter, but they should not be shorter than 6½".*

3. If making a diagonal pocket to accommodate a variety of different-sized items, trim the top of the pocket diagonally from 9" on one side to 5½" on the other as shown in Figure 1.

Figure 1

Completing the Reversible Walker Bag

1. Fold the top edge of each pocket piece ¼" to the wrong side; press. Fold the pressed edge over ½"; press and stitch to hem edge.

2. Center the shoelaces across the 18" width, 10" from each end on the wrong side of one 18" x 20" piece as shown in Figure 2; pin to hold.

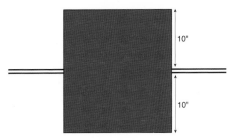

Figure 2

3. Fold the ends of the shoelaces over and pin to the center on the right side of the fabric even with the shoelaces on the back as shown in Figure 3; separate the shoelaces 1" at the edges of the fabric, again referring to Figure 3. Pin in place.

Figure 3

4. Place a hemmed pocket right side up on one end of each 18" x 20" piece as shown in Figure 4; baste to hold in place.

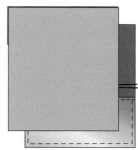

Figure 5

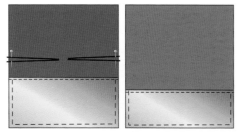

Figure 4

5. Place the pinned units right sides together with pockets on opposite ends as shown in Figure 5.

6. Stitch all around ¼" from edge, leaving a 6" opening along one bottom edge; secure seams at pocket tops and shoelaces for added strength.

7. Trim corners; turn right side out through opening. Press edges flat.

8. Press seam at opening to the inside.

9. Topstitch all around, stitching ¼" across bottom of pockets and ½" along the long edges as shown in Figure 6, closing the pressed opening at the same time. Backstitch over the pocket tops and shoelaces for added strength.

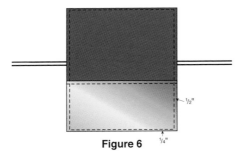

Figure 6   ¼"

10. Mark a line 4½" from one side edge and 5½" from the remaining side edge on each pocket using a water-soluble marker. *Note: The number and size of the pockets may vary depending on the user's needs.*

11. Stitch on marked lines to make pocket sections as shown in Figure 7; backstitch over upper corners and bottom for added strength.

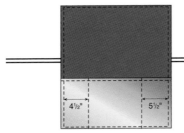

Figure 7

12. Fold the bag over the bar of a walker and tie to legs to use as shown in Figure 8. ◆

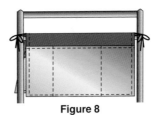

Figure 8

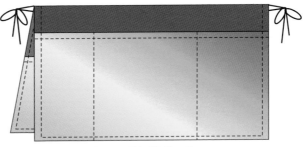

Reversible Walker Bag
Placement Diagram 17½" x 19½"

Hints

If a pocket section is too tall, stitch across the pocket section at desired distance from the bottom of the bag to raise the bottom and make a shorter pocket.

For a wider walker, use longer shoelaces.

Make bags for each season or holiday to brighten someone's day.

Fish Pocket Purse

Little girls will love this fun, whimsical purse.

DESIGN BY NANCY VASILCHIK

PROJECT NOTES

Have some fun experimenting with the special feet that came with your sewing machine. Add some detailed machine stitches or use up some odds and ends of trim to create this fun purse. It is the perfect beach accessory to hold lotions and sunglasses.

PROJECT SPECIFICATIONS

Skill Level: Beginner
Purse Size: 8¾" x 7¾"

MATERIALS

- 1 fat quarter lining fabric (lime green solid)
- 1 fat quarter body fabric (gold tonal)
- 1 fat quarter fish pocket fabric (lime green mottled)
- Scrap red felt (lips)
- Scraps for fins (blue and lavender)
- All-purpose thread to match fabrics
- Assorted colors rayon thread
- ¼ yard medium-weight fusible interfacing
- ¼ yard lightweight tear-off fabric stabilizer
- 45" coordinating cording for handle
- Narrow trims—sequins, cord, ribbon or string of 3–4mm pearls
- ¾" button for eye
- Water-soluble fabric marker
- Basic sewing tools and supplies

OPTIONAL MACHINE SEWING FEET

- Piping foot
- Fancy trim foot
- Open-toe foot
- Mini bead foot
- 7-hole cord foot
- Cording foot
- Button sew-on foot

Completing the Pocket

1. Prepare patterns for pocket, body, fins and lips using patterns given. Set aside body, fin and lips patterns.

2. Trace the pocket shape and tail placement line onto the right side of the pocket fabric using the water-soluble fabric marker; do not cut out. Place stabilizer under fabric.

3. Sew piping to the curved line opposite the tail with raw edge of piping facing outer edge away from tail.

4. Draw four lines following curve of the pocket top, starting the first line 1¼" from piped edge and spacing the lines 1" apart as shown in Figure 1.

5. Draw five lines on the tail section, again referring to Figure 1. Sew a decorative stitch or trim on each of five lines on the tail starting at the last curved line and allowing for a ¼" seam allowance.

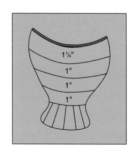

Figure 1

6. Place selected trims on the marked lines and stitch in place or use multiple fancy stitches, using your machine. Extend stitches ¼" beyond marked pocket edge into seam allowance; extend only the base string of the pearls and sequins into the seam allowance area.

7. Cut out the embellished fish pocket along outside traced lines as shown in Figure 2.

Figure 2

8. Place the embellished pocket right sides together with the pocket lining; stitch together along piping stitching line only. Clip curve, turn lining to inside and press edge flat. Pin unstitched edges together to secure; set aside.

Completing the Fish Front

1. Cut body, fin and lip pieces as directed on pattern. Apply fusible interfacing pieces to the wrong side of the body pieces.

2. Stack a body piece and pocket piece right sides up matching edges. Lay a reversed body lining piece right sides together with the layers; pin and stitch a ¼" seam all around, leaving a 4" opening on one fin side of the unit.

3. Clip curves; turn right side out through the 4" opening and press edges flat to complete the fish front unit.

4. Place a reversed body piece and body lining piece right sides together; stitch all around, leaving an opening to turn.

5. Clip curves; turn right side out and press edges flat to complete the fish back unit.

6. Turn opening edges of both units in ¼"; hand-stitch openings closed. Set aside.

7. Add fancy stitches to the front fin pieces as desired.

8. Place the embellished fin pieces right sides together with the reversed fin pieces; stitch around curved sides, leaving straight edge open. Clip curves; turn right side out. Press edges flat.

9. Pin the fish front unit to the fish back unit with lining sides together; insert fins between layers as marked on pattern for positioning.

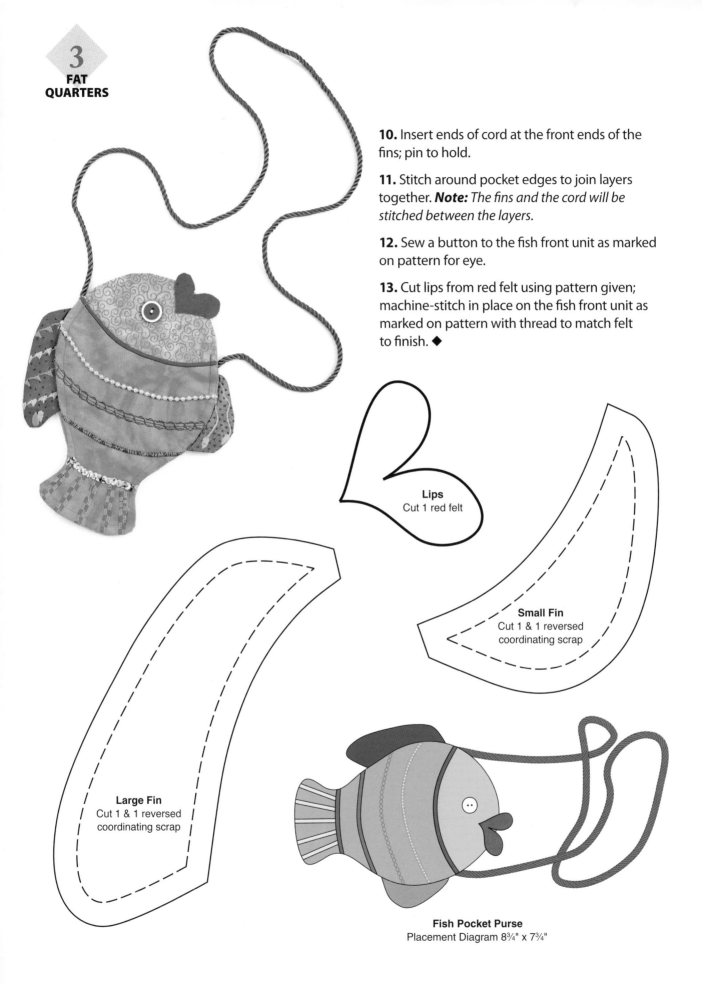

10. Insert ends of cord at the front ends of the fins; pin to hold.

11. Stitch around pocket edges to join layers together. ***Note:*** *The fins and the cord will be stitched between the layers.*

12. Sew a button to the fish front unit as marked on pattern for eye.

13. Cut lips from red felt using pattern given; machine-stitch in place on the fish front unit as marked on pattern with thread to match felt to finish. ◆

Lips
Cut 1 red felt

Small Fin
Cut 1 & 1 reversed
coordinating scrap

Large Fin
Cut 1 & 1 reversed
coordinating scrap

Fish Pocket Purse
Placement Diagram 8¾" x 7¾"

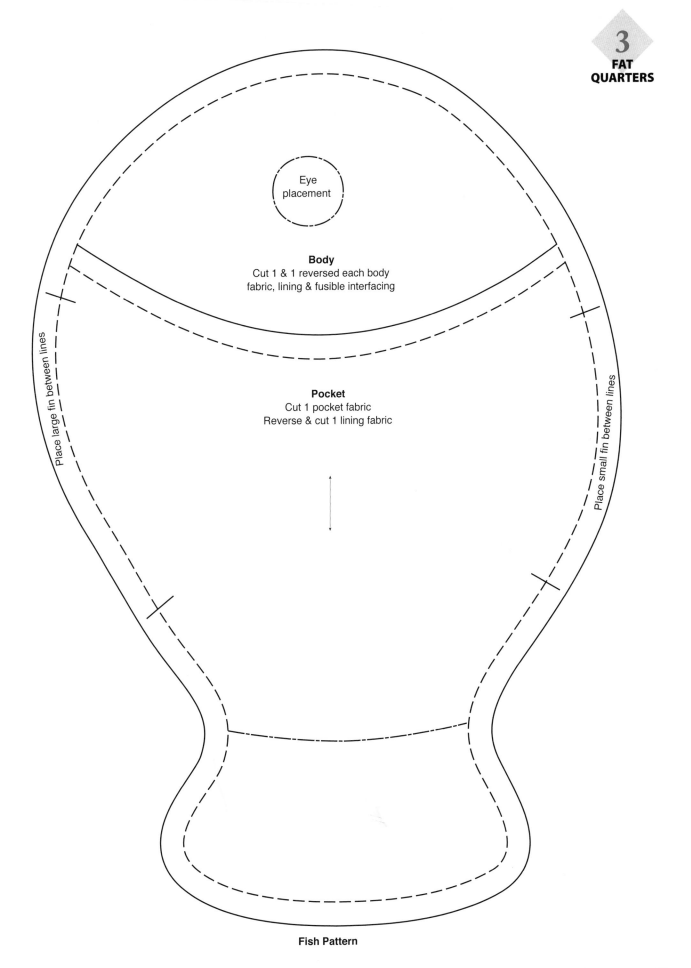

Eye placement

Body
Cut 1 & 1 reversed each body
fabric, lining & fusible interfacing

Place large fin between lines

Pocket
Cut 1 pocket fabric
Reverse & cut 1 lining fabric

Place small fin between lines

Fish Pattern

Topsy-Turvy Table Topper

Use straight lines to create the gentle curves in this clever table topper.

DESIGN BY CONNIE RAND

PROJECT SPECIFICATIONS

Skill Level: Intermediate
Topper Size: 26½" x 26½"

MATERIALS

- 1 fat quarter muslin
- 1 fat quarter black metallic print
- 1 fat quarter black-and-white print
- ⅓ yard black solid
- ½ yard red dot
- Batting 32" x 32"
- Backing 32" x 32"
- All-purpose thread to match fabrics
- Basic sewing tools and supplies

Cutting

1. Prepare templates using patterns given; cut as directed on each piece.

2. Prepare 13 copies each of the A and B paper-piecing patterns using full-size patterns given.

3. Cut two 1½" x 19" H strips and two 1½" x 21" I strips black-and-white print.

4. Cut four 3½" x 21" J strips red dot.

5. Cut four 3½" x 3½" K squares black metallic print.

6. Cut three 2¼" by fabric width strips black solid for binding.

Completing the Topper

1. Cut up two of each paper-piecing pattern to use as templates. ***Note:*** *Because piece 4 cuts across*

pieces 1, 2 and 3, it is not possible to cut all four pieces from just one paper-piecing pattern. Cut fabric pieces in colors as directed for A and B units at least ¼"–½" larger than each numbered space.

2. To complete A sections, lay fabric patch 1 over the space numbered 1 on the unmarked side of the paper pattern. ***Note:*** *Hold the pinned section up to the light and view from the marked side to be sure the fabric patch extends beyond the lines for piece 1.*

3. Set machine stitch length to 25 stitches per inch or 1.5. Pin fabric patch 2 right sides together with piece 1; stitch on the marked side of the paper along the line separating pieces 1 and 2 as shown in Figure 1.

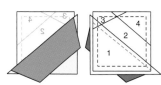

Figure 1   Figure 2

4. Trim seam allowance to ⅛"–¼"; press piece 2 to the right side as shown in Figure 2.

5. Add remaining pieces in numerical order, pressing each piece to the right side before adding the next piece and extending stitching lines into the seam allowance for all edge pieces of the unit. When all pieces are added, trim outer edges of the stitched unit along marked outer line; set aside.

6. Continue paper piecing units until you have completed 12 each A and B units as shown in Figure 3.

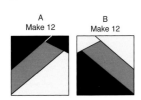

Figure 3

Figure 4

7. Join three each A and B units to make an A-B section as shown in Figure 4; press seams open. Repeat to make four A-B sections.

Figure 5

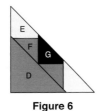

Figure 6

8. Sew E to G as shown in Figure 5; press seams toward E. Repeat to make four E-G units.

9. Sew E to F to G to F to E and add D, pressing seams toward G and D to make a side unit as shown in Figure 6; repeat to make four side units.

10. Join an A-B section, two side units and one E-G unit to complete a corner unit as shown in Figure 7; press seams toward E-G and side units. Repeat to make two corner units.

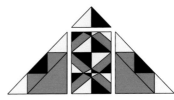

Figure 7

11. Sew an E-G unit to an A-B section as shown in Figure 8; press seams toward E-G unit. Repeat to make two A-B-E-G units.

Figure 8

12. Join the two A-B-E-G units with C to complete the center unit, again referring to Figure 8; press seams toward C.

13. Sew a corner unit to opposite sides of the center unit to complete the pieced center as shown in Figure 9; press seams toward the center unit.

Figure 9

14. Sew H strips to opposite sides and I strips to top and bottom of the pieced center; press seams toward H and I strips.

15. Sew J strips to opposite sides of the pieced center; press seams toward J strips.

16. Sew a K square to each end of each remaining J strip; press seams toward J strips. Sew the J-K strips to top and bottom of the pieced center to complete the pieced top. Press seams toward the J-K strips.

17. Remove all paper patterns.

18. Sandwich batting between the prepared backing and pieced top; pin or baste layers together to hold.

19. Quilt as desired by hand or machine. When quilting is complete, trim excess batting and backing even with edges of the quilted top.

20. Join binding strips on short ends with diagonal seams to make one long strip; trim seams to ¼" and press seams open.

21. Fold binding strip in half wrong sides together along length; press.

22. Sew binding to the right side of the quilted top, mitering corners and overlapping ends; press binding away from edges and turn to the back side. Hand- or machine-stitch in place to finish. ◆

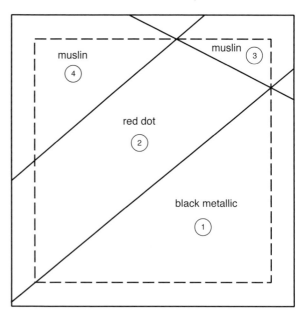

Paper-Piecing Pattern A
Make 14 copies

Paper-Piecing Pattern B
Make 14 copies

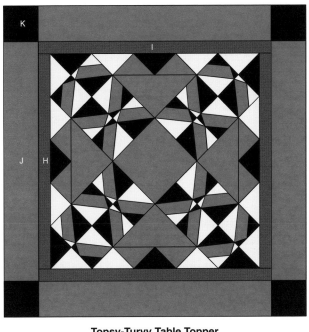

Topsy-Turvy Table Topper
Placement Diagram 26½" x 26½"

C
Cut 1 red dot

Place line on fold

E/F/G
Cut 12 muslin for E, 8 red dot for F
& 8 black metallic print for G

D
Cut 4 red dot

The Maze Table Runner

Use fabric to create the look of a garden maze with this simple runner.

DESIGN BY JULIE WEAVER

PROJECT SPECIFICATIONS

Skill Level: Beginner
Runner Size: 42" x 15"
Block Size: 7" x 9" and 4" x 9"
Number of Blocks: 4 and 2

MATERIALS

• 1 fat quarter mosaic print
• 1 fat quarter cream tonal
• 1 fat quarter teal/brown print
• ⅜ yard green/brown dot
• ⅝ yard brown confetti print
• Batting 50" x 23"
• Backing 50" x 23"
• All-purpose thread to match fabrics
• Basic sewing tools and supplies

Cutting

1. Cut two 3½" x 21" A strips green/brown dot.

2. Cut four 1½" x 21" B strips green/brown dot.

3. Cut three 1" by fabric width L/M strips green/brown dot; subcut one strip into two 11½" M strips. Cut each of remaining two strips 37½" for L.

4. Cut three 3½" x 21" C strips mosaic print.

5. Cut two 2½" x 21" E strips mosaic print.

6. Cut two 1½" x 21" D strips cream tonal.

7. Cut two 5½" x 21" F strips cream tonal.

8. Cut two 1½" x 21" strips cream tonal; subcut strips into four 9½" G strips.

9. Cut two 3½" x 21" H strips teal/brown print.

10. Cut two 2½" x 21" I strips teal/brown print.

11. Cut three 1" by fabric width J/K strips brown confetti print; subcut one strip into two 10½" K strips. Cut each of remaining two strips 36½" for J.

12. Cut three 2½" by fabric width N/O strips brown confetti print; subcut one strip into two 15½" O strips. Cut each of remaining two strips 38½" for N.

13. Cut three 2¼" by fabric width strips brown confetti print for binding.

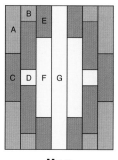

Maze
7" x 9" Block
Make 4

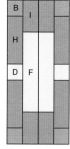

Sashing
4" x 9" Block
Make 2

Completing the Maze Blocks

1. Sew a C strip between two A strips along length; press seams toward C strip.

2. Subcut the A-C strip into eight 1½" A-C units as shown in Figure 1.

Figure 1

3. Sew an F strip between two E strips along length; press seams toward E strips.

4. Subcut the E-F strip set into eight 1½" E-F units as shown in Figure 2.

Figure 2

5. Sew a D strip between two C strips and two B strips along length to make a B-C-D strip set; press seams toward C and then B.

6. Subcut the B-C-D strip set into eight 1½" B-C-D units as shown in Figure 3.

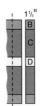

Figure 3

7. To complete one Maze block, sew an E-F unit to opposite side of G as shown in Figure 4; press seams toward G.

Figure 4

8. Sew a B-C-D unit to opposite sides of the stitched unit, again referring to Figure 4; press seams toward the E-F units.

9. Sew an A-C unit to opposite sides of the stitched unit, again referring to Figure 4; press seams toward the A-C units to complete one Maze block referring to block drawing.

10. Repeat steps 7–9 to complete four Maze blocks.

Completing the Sashing Blocks

1. Sew a D strip between two H strips and two B strips along length; press seams toward H and then B.

2. Subcut the B-D-H strip set into four 1½" B-D-H units as shown in Figure 5.

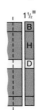

Figure 5

3. Sew an F strip between two I strips along length; press seams toward I.

4. Subcut the F-I strip set into four 1½" F-I units as shown in Figure 6.

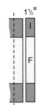

Figure 6

5. To complete one Sashing block, join two F-I units along length; press seam to one side.

6. Sew a B-D-H unit to opposite sides of the F-I units; press seams toward the F-I units to complete one Sashing block referring to the block drawing.

7. Repeat steps 5 and 6 to complete a second Sashing block.

Completing the Runner

1. Join two Maze blocks along the 9½" sides; add a Sashing block to each side of the stitched unit and add another Maze block to each end; press seams in one direction to complete the pieced center.

2. Sew a J strip to opposite long sides and K strips to the short ends of the pieced center; press seams toward J and K strips.

3. Sew an L strip to opposite long sides and M strips to the short ends of the pieced center; press seams toward L and M strips.

4. Sew an N strip to opposite long sides and O strips to the short ends of the pieced center; press seams toward N and O strips.

5. Sandwich the batting between the completed top and prepared backing; pin or baste layers together.

6. Quilt as desired by hand or machine. Join binding strips on short ends with diagonal seams to make one long strip; trim seams to ¼" and press seams open.

7. Fold binding strip in half wrong sides together along length; press.

8. Sew binding to the right side of the runner, matching raw edges, mitering corners and overlapping ends; press binding away from runner edges and turn to the back side. Hand- or machine-stitch in place to finish. ◆

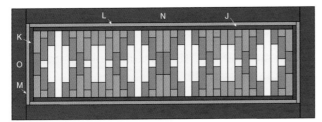

The Maze Table Runner
Placement Diagram 42" x 15"

China Blue Topper

The unique hexagon shape and blue floral fabrics join in adding a lovely traditional touch to your table.

DESIGN BY JULIE WEAVER

PROJECT SPECIFICATIONS

Skill Level: Beginner
Topper Size: 36" x 36"
Block Size: 9" x 9"
Number of Blocks: 4

MATERIALS

- 1 fat quarter each light and medium blue prints
- 1 fat quarter white/blue dot
- ½ yard white/blue floral
- ⅔ yard small dark blue floral print
- ⅔ yard large dark blue floral
- Batting 44" x 44"
- Backing 44" x 44"
- All-purpose thread to match fabrics
- Quilting thread
- Basic sewing tools and supplies

Cutting

1. Cut one 4¼" x 21" strip white/blue dot; subcut strip into four 4¼" B squares.

2. Cut one 2⅜" x 21" strip white/blue dot; subcut strip into eight 2⅜" G squares.

3. Cut four 2" x 21" strips white/blue dot; subcut strips into (32) 2" F squares.

4. Cut one 3⅞" by fabric width strip large dark blue floral; subcut strip into eight 3⅞" D squares.

5. Cut four 4" by fabric width strips large dark blue floral; subcut each strip into one 15" L strip and one 25" M strip.

6. Cut one 2⅜" by fabric width strip small dark blue floral; subcut strip into eight 2⅜" H squares.

7. Cut four 1½" by fabric width strips small dark blue floral; subcut strips into eight 21" K strips.

8. Cut four 2¼" by fabric width strips small dark blue floral for binding.

9. Cut two 3½" x 21" strips medium blue print; subcut strips into (16) 2" E rectangles.

10. Cut one 4¼" x 21" strip light blue print; subcut strip into four 4¼" C squares.

11. Cut one 14" by fabric width strip white/blue floral; subcut strip into one 14" square, one 9½" x 9½" J square and four 3½" x 3½" A squares. Cut the 14" x 14" square on both diagonals to make four I triangles.

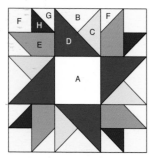

China Blue 1
9" x 9" Block
Make 2

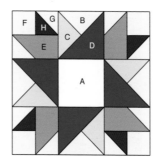

China Blue 2
9" x 9" Block
Make 2

Completing the Blocks

1. Draw a diagonal line on the wrong side of each B square.

2. Place a marked B square right sides together with a C square and sew ¼" on each side of the marked line as shown in Figure 1.

Figure 1

3. Cut apart on the drawn line and press C to the right side to complete two B-C units as shown in Figure 2.

Figure 2

4. Repeat steps 2 and 3 to complete eight B-C units.

5. Draw a diagonal line across the seam on the wrong side of each B-C unit as shown in Figure 3.

Figure 3   **Figure 4**

6. Place each of these squares right sides together with a D square and sew ¼" on each side of the marked lines as shown in Figure 4.

7. Cut apart on the marked lines, and press D to the right side to make eight B-C-D units and eight reversed B-C-D units as shown in Figure 5.

Figure 5

8. Repeat step 1 with G squares and steps 2 and 3 with the marked G squares and H to complete 16 G-H units as shown in Figure 6.

Figure 6

9. Draw a diagonal line on the wrong side of each F square.

10. Place F right sides together on one end of E and stitch on the marked line as shown in Figure 7.

Figure 7

11. Trim seam to ¼" and press F to the right side to complete an E-F unit, again referring to Figure 7.

12. Repeat steps 10 and 11 to make 16 E-F units.

13. To complete one China Blue 1 block, select one A square and four each B-C-D units, F squares, G-H units and E-F units.

14. Sew F to the H side of a G-H unit as shown in Figure 8; press seam toward F. Add an E-F unit to complete one corner unit as shown in Figure 9; press seam toward the E-F unit. Repeat to make four corner units.

Figure 8   **Figure 9**

15. Sew a B-C-D unit between two corner units to make a row as shown in Figure 10; repeat to make two rows. Press seams toward the B-C-D units.

Figure 10

16. Sew an A square between two B-C-D units to make the center row as shown in Figure 11; press seams toward A.

Figure 11

17. Sew the center row between the two previously pieced rows to complete the China Blue 1 block; press seams toward the center row.

18. Repeat steps 13–17 to complete a second China Blue 1 block.

19. Repeat steps 13–17 with the reversed B-C-D units referring to Figure 12 to complete two China Blue 2 blocks.

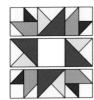

Figure 12

Completing the Top

1. Sew a J square between the two China Blue 2 blocks to make the center row as shown in Figure 13; press seams toward J.

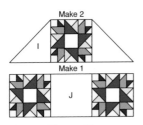

Make 2

Make 1

Figure 13

2. Sew an I triangle to opposite sides of each China Blue 1 block to make two I rows as shown in Figure 13; press seams toward I.

3. Sew an I row to opposite sides of the center row to complete the pieced center; press seams toward the center row.

4. Center and sew a K strip to the I sides of the pieced center as shown in Figure 14; press seams toward the K strips.

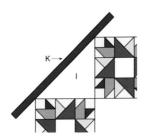

Figure 14

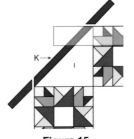

Figure 15

5. Trim excess K strips at each end even with the blocks using a straightedge as shown in Figure 15.

6. Repeat steps 4 and 5 on the block sides of the pieced center.

7. Repeat steps 4 and 5 with L strips first, and then M strips, to complete the pieced top; press seams toward L and M strips.

Completing the Table Topper

1. Sandwich the batting between the completed top and prepared backing; pin or baste layers together.

2. Quilt as desired by hand or machine. When quilting is complete, trim batting and backing even with edges of the quilted top.

3. Join binding strips on short ends with diagonal seams to make one long strip; trim seams to ¼" and press seams open.

4. Fold binding strip in half wrong sides together along length; press.

5. Sew binding to the right side of the topper, matching raw edges, mitering corners and overlapping ends; press binding away from topper edges and turn to the back side. Hand- or machine-stitch in place to finish. ◆

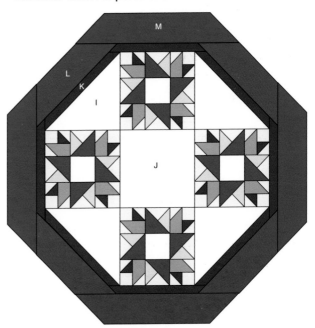

China Blue Topper
Placement Diagram 36" x 36"

Holly Table Mat

Place a beautiful centerpiece or poinsettia plant on this mat to add a festive touch to your holiday table.

DESIGN BY BARBARA A. CLAYTON

PROJECT SPECIFICATIONS

Skill Level: Intermediate
Table Mat Size: Approximately 20" x 16½"

MATERIALS

- 1 fat quarter red dot
- 1 fat quarter medium green mottled
- 1 fat quarter narrow red-and-white stripe
- 1 fat quarter red backing fabric
- ½ yard dark green tonal
- Batting 21" x 18"
- All-purpose thread to match fabrics
- White quilting thread
- .004 clear nylon thread
- Clear tape
- Plain white paper
- Water-soluble glue stick
- Water-soluble marking pen
- ¼" bias bar
- Basic sewing tools and supplies

Cutting

1. Prepare patterns for mat pieces; tape together on A-B line. Trace the pattern four times on plain white paper; cut out and tape together to make the pattern. Pin the paper pattern on the dark green tonal and cut out. Remove pattern.

2. Trim the pattern to the inside line; pin the trimmed pattern on the red dot and cut out.

3. Cut 1" bias strips from the narrow red-and-white stripe to equal 70"; join on short ends to make one long bias strip as shown in Figure 1.

Figure 1

4. Cut 1½"-wide bias strips dark green tonal to total 80"; join on short ends to make one long strip.

Preparing the Holly Leaves

1. Trace the holly leaf patterns 10 times and the berry-cluster pattern 12 times on the plain white paper; reverse the holly leaf pattern and trace 10 times. Cut out on traced lines. **Note:** *You may layer the paper and cut multiple pieces at one time.*

2. Lay the holly-leaf paper patterns on the wrong side of the medium green mottled and cut out, leaving a ¼" margin around each one.

3. Repeat step 2 with the berry-cluster patterns on the remaining red dot. **Note:** *Fussy-cut pieces between dots to make berry clumps all red.*

4. Center and pin a corresponding paper pattern on the wrong side of each fabric shape; clip points and curves almost to the paper as shown in Figure 2.

Figure 2

5. Rub the glue stick along the edge of the paper pattern a little at a time and fold the fabric edges up and over the edge, gluing to the paper; repeat for all appliqué shapes.

Completing the Table Mat

1. Center the red dot mat piece right side up on the dark green tonal piece; baste to hold in place.

2. Fold the prepared bias strip in half wrong sides together along length; stitch a scant ¼" seam allowance along the raw edge. Trim seam to ⅛"; insert the ¼" bias bar inside the strip and rotate seam to the center back of the bar as shown in Figure 3. Press seam open and slide the bar along the whole strip to create a narrow finished bias strip.

Figure 3

3. Starting at a right-angle corner of the red center, place and pin the bias strip, right side up, over the raw edge between the red and green layers, mitering the inner and outer corners and curving around each curve, following the edge design.

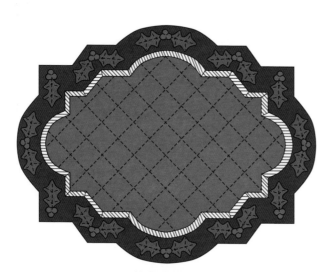

Holly Table Mat
Placement Diagram 20" x 16½"

4. Slipstitch binding in place on each side of the strip; end by trimming off the excess strip, turning under the end ¼" on a diagonal, to finish the mitered look of the beginning right angle corner as shown in Figure 4. ***Note:*** *You may machine-stitch the bias strip in place with clear nylon thread, using a narrow blind-hem stitch.*

Figure 4

5. Turn the stitched mat with the back side up and carefully cut away the center green fabric underneath the red center to within ¼" of the stitching for the bias strip to reduce bulk as shown in Figure 5.

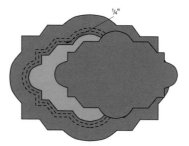

Figure 5

6. Arrange and pin the holly leaves and berry clusters in the dark green border area of the candle mat referring to the Placement Diagram for positioning; hand-stitch each shape in place using thread to match fabric or machine-stitch with clear nylon thread using a narrow blind-hem stitch.

7. Turn the stitched mat with the back side up; cut a slit through the back of each appliqué shape. Wet the appliqué area with a sponge and reach into the slit and carefully pull out the paper; let dry.

8. Draw diagonal-grid quilting lines in the center red area 1¾" apart in both directions and the holly-leaf vein quilting lines and berry-design lines using the water-soluble marking pen.

9. Sandwich the batting between the completed top and red fat-quarter backing; pin or baste layers together.

10. Machine-stitch the layers together ¼" from outer edges and close to both edges of the narrow red-and-white stripe bias strip using clear nylon thread; remove pins or basting.

11. Hand-quilt marked lines and around all the leaf and berry pieces with white quilting thread. Trim batting and backing even with the quilted top.

12. Press one long edge of the dark green tonal bias strip ¼" to the wrong side. Starting at a right-angle corner, stitch binding to mat matching raw edges and mitering inner and outer corners and curving around each curve, ending by trimming away the excess and folding the edge over ¼".

13. Fold binding to the back side; hand-stitch in place to finish. ◆

Berry Cluster
Cut as directed

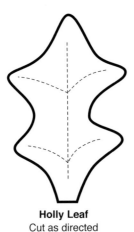

Holly Leaf
Cut as directed

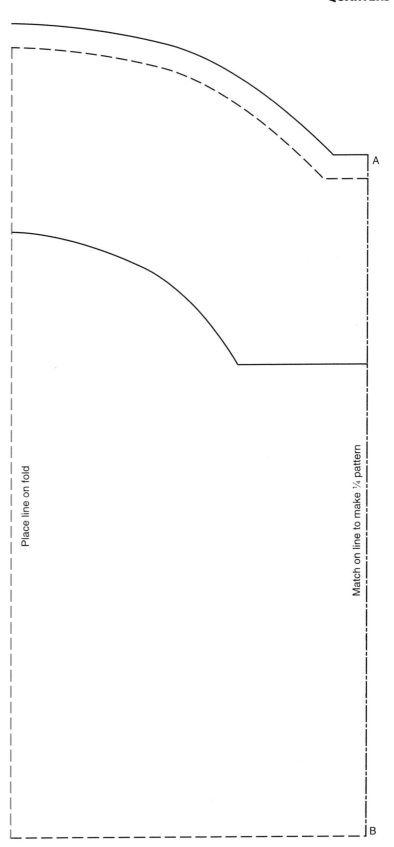

A

B

Place line on fold

Match on line to make ¼ pattern

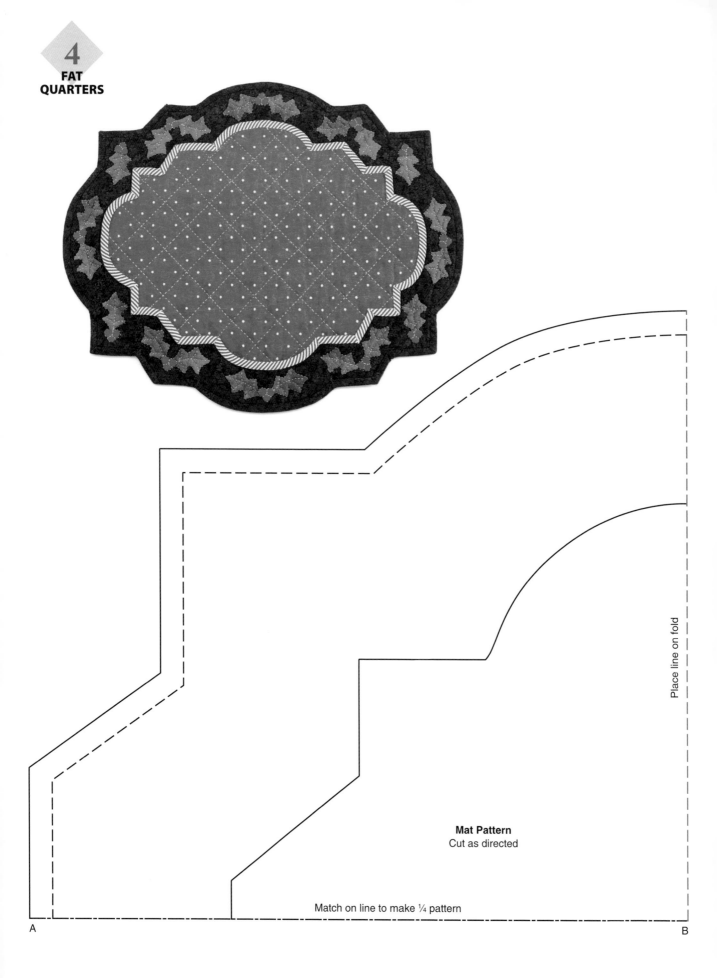

Place line on fold

Mat Pattern
Cut as directed

Match on line to make ¼ pattern

A   B

Autumn Place Mats

Add a touch of autumn to your table with these quick-to-stitch place mats.

DESIGN BY CAROLYN S. VAGTS

PROJECT SPECIFICATIONS

Skill Level: Beginner
Place Mat Size: 19" x 14"

MATERIALS FOR 2 PLACE MATS

- 4 fat quarters coordinating autumn-colored batiks
- ⅞ yard brown batik
- 2 (25" x 20") pieces insulated batting
- 2 (25" x 20") backing pieces
- All-purpose thread to match fabrics
- Quilting thread
- Basic sewing tools and supplies

Cutting

1. Cut one 11½" by fabric width strip brown batik; subcut into two 16½" A rectangles.

2. Cut two 2" by fabric width strips brown batik; subcut into two 11½" B strips and two 19½" C strips.

3. Cut four 2¼" by fabric width strips brown batik for binding.

4. Cut two or three 1½" x 21" D strips from each of the four coordinating autumn-colored batiks. Cut each strip into two 10½" strips.

Completing the Place Mats

1. Measure and mark 6" on each side of the top left corner of one A rectangle as shown in

Figure 1. Repeat on the bottom right corner, again referring to Figure 1.

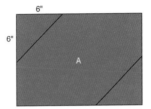

Figure 1

2. Connect the marks to make lines; cut along marked lines to make angled corners as shown in Figure 2.

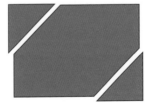

Figure 2

3. Select one of the D strips and place right sides together along one angled end of A as shown in Figure 3; stitch. Press strip to the right side.

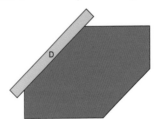

Figure 3

4. Repeat step 3 on the opposite corner using the same-colored D strip.

5. Continue adding D strips on each corner until there are five D strips on each corner as shown in Figure 4. ***Note:*** *Each added strip will be shorter than the previous strip.*

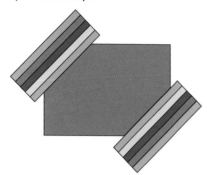

Figure 4

6. When stitching and pressing is complete, trim strip ends even with edges of A to make square corners as shown in Figure 5.

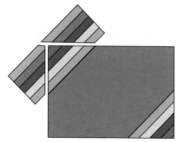

Figure 5

7. Sew B strips to short ends and C strips to opposite long sides to complete one place mat top; press seams toward B and C strips. Repeat to make a second place mat top.

8. Sandwich a batting piece between a place mat top and a backing piece; pin or baste layers together to hold. Repeat with second place mat top.

9. Quilt as desired by hand or machine. When quilting is complete, trim batting and backing even with edges of the place mat tops.

10. Join binding strips on short ends with diagonal seams to make one long strip; trim seams to ¼" and press seams open.

11. Fold binding strip in half wrong sides together along length; press.

12. With raw edges even, sew binding to the top side of place mat, using a ¼" seam allowance, mitering corners and overlapping ends; press binding away from place mat edges and turn to the back side. Hand- or machine-stitch in place to finish. ◆

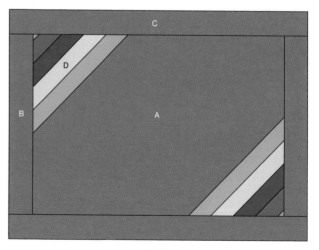

Autumn Place Mat
Placement Diagram 19" x 14"

Petal Pillow

Flower power is not just a phrase from the 1960s and 1970s—flower shapes such as this one are popular again today.

DESIGN BY CONNIE KAUFFMAN

PROJECT SPECIFICATIONS

Skill Level: Beginner
Pillow Size: Approximately 22" x 22"

MATERIALS

- 1 fat quarter red/black/white print
- 1 fat quarter coordinating red print
- 1 fat quarter yellow/black/white print
- 1 fat quarter coordinating yellow print
- ⅓ yard white microfleece
- 36" x 22" polyester batting
- White all-purpose thread
- Polyester fiberfill
- Basic sewing tools and supplies

Cutting

1. Prepare template for petal using pattern given.

2. Draw a 10"-diameter circle on a piece of paper; cut out to make a pattern.

3. Trace the circle pattern twice onto the wrong side of the white microfleece; cut out on drawn line. Shake the pieces over a waste basket to remove all shedding fibers.

Completing the Pillow

1. Trace six petal shapes onto the wrong side of the coordinating yellow print.

2. Place the batting on a work surface. Place the red/black/white print right side up on top of the batting and the coordinating yellow print right side down on the red/black/white print; pin-baste layers together.

3. Sew ¼" inside the marked lines on the wrong side of the coordinating yellow print, leaving bottom edge open.

4. Cut out shapes along marked lines; trim batting close to stitching.

5. Turn each petal shape right side out through openings; press edges flat.

6. Topstitch ½" from edges around each petal.

7. Repeat steps 1–6 with yellow/black/white print and coordinating red print.

8. Fold the paper circle in half and then in thirds so that the circle is divided equally into six pie shapes as shown in Figure 1.

Figure 1

Figure 2

the folded line of the circle pattern referring to Figure 3; pin to secure.

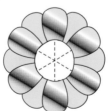

Figure 3

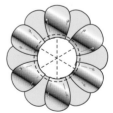

Figure 4

9. Lay each of the red/black/white print petals yellow side up with the inside edges ¼" inside each of the six sections of the paper circle as shown in Figure 2; pin to secure.

10. Lay each of the yellow/black/white print petals with the yellow side up, centering each petal on

11. Pin petals together where they overlap. Machine-baste ¼" from the edge of the petals as shown in Figure 4.

12. Lay a white circle right side up over the center of the petals; turn under edges ¼" and pin to hold.

13. Machine-stitch close to the edge of the circle through all layers. Remove paper circle.

14. Turn the pillow over and repeat steps 12 and 13, leaving a 3" opening.

15. Insert polyester fiberfill through the opening to desired fullness; stitch opening closed to finish pillow. ◆

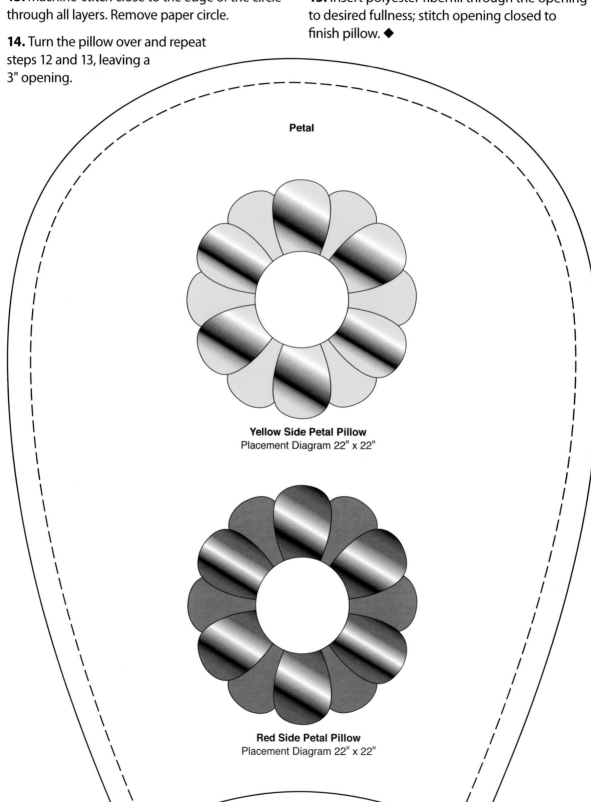

Petal

Yellow Side Petal Pillow
Placement Diagram 22" x 22"

Red Side Petal Pillow
Placement Diagram 22" x 22"

Chicks Pocket Pillow

Stuff the pockets on this colorful pillow
with surprises for your little one.

DESIGN BY PHYLLIS DOBBS

PROJECT SPECIFICATIONS

Skill Level: Beginner
Pillow Size: 20½" x 18"

MATERIALS

- 1 fat quarter blue tonal
- 1 fat quarter each red and green prints
- 1 fat quarter coordinating stripe
- ¾ yard gold print
- Muslin lining (2) 24" x 22"
- Batting (2) 24" x 22"
- All-purpose thread to match fabrics
- Blendable multicolored cotton quilting thread
- ½ yard fusible web
- 3 assorted blue or green ¼"–⁵⁄₁₆" round beads
- 18" x 22" pillow insert
- Basic sewing tools and supplies

Cutting

1. Cut one 10½" x 21" A rectangle
coordinating stripe.

2. Cut one 21" by fabric width strip gold print;
subcut into one 18½" backing rectangle and two
4½" x 21" B rectangles.

3. Cut one 5½" x 12½" C piece each blue tonal and
green and red prints for pockets.

4. Trace appliqué shape onto the paper side of the
fusible web as directed on pattern; cut out shapes,
leaving a margin around each one.

5. Fuse shapes to the wrong side of the gold
print; cut out shapes on traced lines. Remove
paper backing.

Completing the Pillow

1. Fold a C piece in half along length with wrong
sides together to make a 5½" x 6¼" rectangle;
crease folded edge.

2. Unfold the C piece and center and fuse a chick
shape with head toward the creased line as shown
in Figure 1.

c

Figure 1

3. Using a narrowly spaced zigzag stitch, sew
around the edges of the chick shape using thread
to match chick.

4. Refold the appliquéd C rectangle with right
sides together; sew around raw edge, leaving a
3" opening on one side.

5. Trim corners and turn the stitched C piece right
side out; press edges flat at seams.

6. Press the seam allowance to the inside of the
opening and hand-stitch closed.

7. Sew a bead in place as marked on pattern for
eye to complete one pocket.

8. Repeat steps 1–7 to complete two
more pockets.

9. Center and pin one pocket on A as shown in Figure 2; topstitch ⅛" from side and bottom edges, leaving top edge open. ***Note:*** *Because A is a stripe, be sure that the edge of the pocket is parallel to a stripe line.*

Figure 2

10. Arrange, pin and stitch the remaining two pockets on each side of A as in step 9, leaving 1" between pockets as shown in Figure 3.

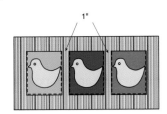

Figure 3

11. Sew a B rectangle to opposite long sides of A to complete the pillow top; press seams toward B.

12. Sandwich batting between the muslin lining and the completed top; quilt as desired by hand or machine.

13. When quilting is complete, trim muslin and batting edges even with the quilted top.

14. Place the pillow backing right sides together with the quilted top; stitch all around, leaving a 16" opening on one end.

15. Clip corners; turn right side out. Press edges flat and opening seams to the inside.

16. Insert pillow form; hand-stitch opening closed to complete the pillow. ◆

Chicks Pocket Pillow
Placement Diagram 20½" x 18"

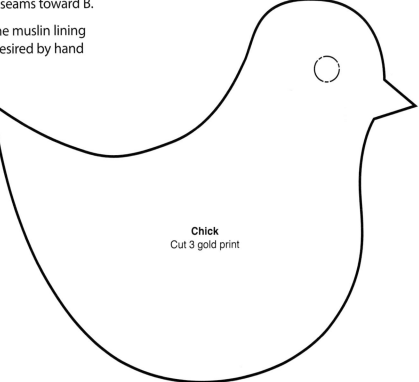

Chick
Cut 3 gold print

One, Two, Three Little Chickens

Whether hung from a bedroom door or set on their bed, fun is just around the corner when imagination is left up to the kids.

DESIGN BY LORINE MASON

PROJECT SPECIFICATIONS

Skill Level: Beginner
Pillow Size: 10½" x 11½"

MATERIALS

- 1 fat quarter each gold and light green tonals
- 1 fat quarter each light aqua and yellow prints
- Scrap aqua tonal
- 5½" x 5½" thin batting
- White all-purpose thread
- ½ yard fusible web
- Polyester fiberfill
- ½ yard ¼"-wide green ribbon
- 3 wooden ice-cream spoons
- ¼" hole punch
- Black fabric pen
- Pinking shears
- Permanent fabric adhesive
- Basic sewing tools and supplies

Cutting

1. Trace roof and chicken pieces onto the paper side of the fusible web using patterns given; do not add seam allowance.

2. Draw a 2½" x 3¼" rectangle on the paper side of the fusible web for upper door.

3. Cut out shapes, leaving a margin around each one.

4. Fuse shapes onto the wrong side of fabrics as directed on patterns for color, fusing upper door rectangle on the gold tonal. Cut out shapes on traced lines. Remove paper backing.

5. Cut one 11" x 12" rectangle each light aqua and yellow prints for barn front and back.

6. Cut one 2" x 6" hinge strip light green tonal.

7. Cut one 5" x 5" square each light aqua print and gold tonal for pocket and pocket lining.

8. Cut one each 5½" x 5½" square yellow print and gold tonal for barn door and lining.

9. Cut one 2" x 10" strip aqua tonal for handle.

Completing the Pillow

1. Place the roof piece right side up on the barn piece, aligning top and side bottom edges as shown in Figure 1; fuse in place. Trim excess barn pieces from the top of the roof edges again referring to Figure 1.

Figure 1

2. Machine buttonhole-stitch along inside and bottom edge of the roof piece.

3. Topstitch lines 1" apart from the bottom of the barn front to the roof edge as shown in Figure 2.

Figure 2

4. Center the upper barn door piece on the barn front piece 1½" below the roof and fuse in place as shown in Figure 3.

Figure 3

5. Stitch in place as in step 2. Add straight stitches from corner to corner to make an X.

6. Place the 5" x 5" pocket and pocket lining pieces right sides together; stitch around three sides. Clip corners, turn right side out and press edges flat.

7. Center the pocket on the bottom of the barn front, matching raw edges; stitch in place along side edges of pocket as in step 2.

8. Lay the two 5½" x 5½" barn door and lining squares right sides together on the batting square; stitch around outside edge, leaving left-side edge open. Turn right side out; press edges flat.

9. Topstitch ¼" from edge around the three stitched sides. Stitch an X from corner to corner to complete the barn door.

10. Center and pin the door ¼" above the bottom edge of the pillow front, over the pocket.

11. Fold the 2" x 6" hinge piece in half with right sides together along length; stitch along the long side.

12. Turn right side out and press with seam centered. Turn under top edge ¼".

13. Center the hinge over the left raw-edge side of the barn door; topstitch around the top and sides as shown in Figure 4.

Figure 4

14. Prepare handle strip as in steps 11 and 12, except do not turn under top edge.

15. Topstitch close to edge along both long sides.

16. Pin handle to the top edge of the barn ¼" in from each side edge as shown in Figure 5; machine-baste to hold in place.

Figure 5

17. Place the pillow front and back right sides together; stitch around the outside edge leaving a 3" opening along one side. Turn right side out and press edges flat.

18. Stuff pillow with polyester fiberfill through opening as desired for fullness.

19. Turn opening edges ¼" to the inside; hand-stitch opening closed to finish pillow.

Completing the Chicken Puppets

1. Fuse the remaining aqua and yellow prints with wrong sides together for puppet backings.

2. Arrange the previously cut chicken pieces on the aqua side of the fused fabric layers as shown in Figure 6, leaving at least ¾" between motifs;

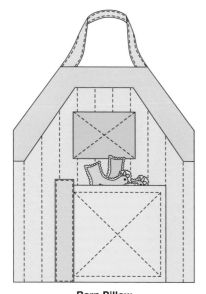

Barn Pillow
Placement Diagram 10½" x 11½"

Chicken Puppets
Placement Diagram

when satisfied with motif placement, fuse in place to make one small and two large chickens.

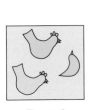

Figure 6

Figure 7

3. Using the pinking shears, cut around the edge of each chicken motif, leaving a ¼" border all around each one as shown in Figure 7.

4. Using black fabric pen, add an eye to each chicken as marked on patterns.

5. Position and glue the wooden sticks to the back side of each chicken to make puppets.

6. Punch a hole in the center of the bottom of each stick ¼" from bottom edge.

7. Cut the green ribbon into three 6" lengths; fold each piece in half and thread the doubled ends through the holes, inserting ends into the loops as shown in Figure 8. Pull tight.

Figure 8

8. Insert the chicken puppets into the pocket under the barn door to finish; let the fun begin! ◆

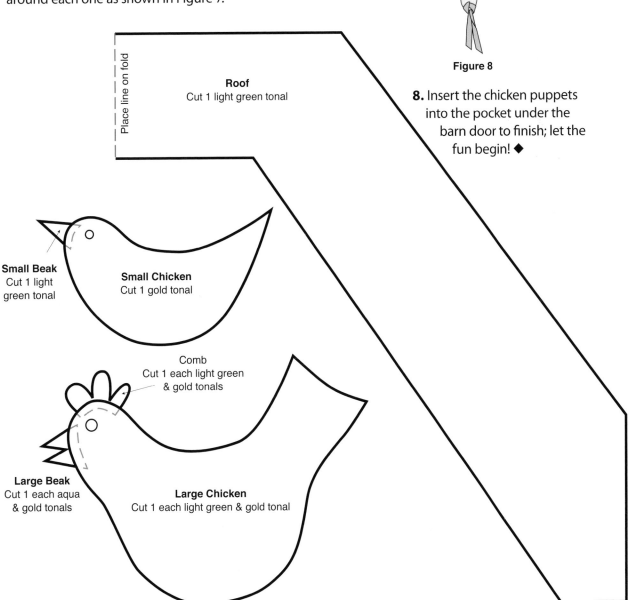

Place line on fold

Roof
Cut 1 light green tonal

Small Beak
Cut 1 light green tonal

Small Chicken
Cut 1 gold tonal

Comb
Cut 1 each light green & gold tonals

Large Beak
Cut 1 each aqua & gold tonals

Large Chicken
Cut 1 each light green & gold tonal

"Life of the Party" Dog Coat

Dress your dog in the latest style with this comfy, easy-to-stitch coat. Tips on resizing the coat to fit your dog are included.

DESIGN BY PHYLLIS DOBBS

PROJECT SPECIFICATIONS

Skill Level: Beginner
Coat Size: 15" x 21" for a medium-size dog

MATERIALS

- 1 fat quarter green dog print
- 1 fat quarter orange dog-bones print
- 1 fat quarter aqua bird print
- 1 fat quarter fuchsia dog-bones print
- 1 (9¼" x 9¼") dog preprinted panel
- Batting 21" x 27"
- Neutral-color all-purpose thread
- Multicolored quilting thread
- ½ yard 16"-wide double-sided fusible web
- Basic sewing tools and supplies

Cutting

1. Prepare trimming templates for neck and tail using the full-size patterns given.

2. Trim the green dog print fat quarter to 15½" x 21½"; fold in half with right sides together along length. Place the trimming templates at each end on the folded edge as shown in Figure 1; mark and trim to complete the A piece, again referring to Figure 1.

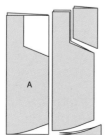

Figure 1

3. Repeat step 2 with the orange dog-bones print to make the backing.

4. Cut five 2½" x 21" strips aqua bird print for ruffle.

5. Cut three 1¾" x 18" aqua bird print for ties.

6. Cut three 1¾" x 18" fuchsia dog-bones print for ties.

7. Trim the preprinted panel with ⅜" extra around panel to turn to the back side.

Completing the Dog Coat

1. Fold and press the extra ⅜" around the dog panel to the wrong side.

2. Cut a square of fusible web ¼" smaller than the pressed dog panel all around; fuse to the wrong side of the dog panel over the turned-under edges referring to manufacturer's instructions. Remove paper backing.

3. Center and fuse the dog panel to the green A piece with the top of the panel toward the neck area of A referring to Figure 2.

Figure 2

4. Join the ruffle strips on short ends to make one long strip; press seams open. Trim strip to make two 46½" ruffle strips. Fold short raw edges of each strip ¼" to the wrong side.

5. Fold a ruffle strip with wrong sides together along length to make a long double-layered strip.

6. Sew a line of machine gathering stitches a scant ¼" from the raw edge of the strip and gather to 21".

7. Repeat steps 5 and 6 to make two ruffles.

8. Fold a tie strip in half with rights sides together along length; sew across one end and along the long raw edge. Clip corners and turn right side out; press flat with seam at one side to complete one tie. Repeat to make three each aqua and fuchsia ties.

Tip

To resize the coat for your dog, measure the distance between the base of the dog's neck and 3" from the tail. Add or subtract from the pattern given so that it fits these measurements. Adjust flaps accordingly, especially for a smaller dog. Measure across the dog, measuring from 2" or 3" above the bottom of the dog to the same point on the other side. Adjust the width of the pattern according to this measurement.

9. Place the orange backing piece right sides up on top of the batting, aligning edges; trim batting even with edges of backing. Pin and baste one tie of each color to the center of the top narrow ends. Pin and baste one tie of each color 7" from each end of the coat as shown in Figure 3, alternating tie colors from one side to the other.

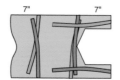

Figure 3

10. Pin and baste one gathered ruffle to each long side on top of ties, aligning raw edges and adjusting gathers as needed to fit as shown in Figure 4.

Figure 4

11. Pin the green fused A piece right sides together with the orange piece, tucking ties and ruffle inside between layers; stitch all around,

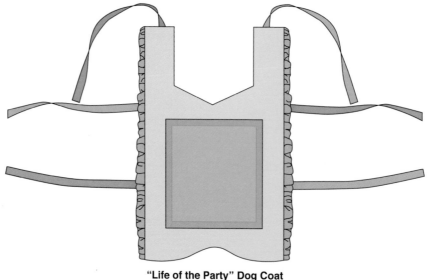

"Life of the Party" Dog Coat
Placement Diagram 15" x 21"

leaving a 4" opening on the back end as shown in Figure 5; clip inside points and trim corners. Turn right side out through opening and press edges flat.

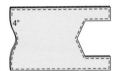

Figure 5

12. Turn opening edges in ¼"; press. Hand- or machine-stitch opening closed.

13. Baste layers together for quilting; machine quilt as desired to complete the dog coat. ◆

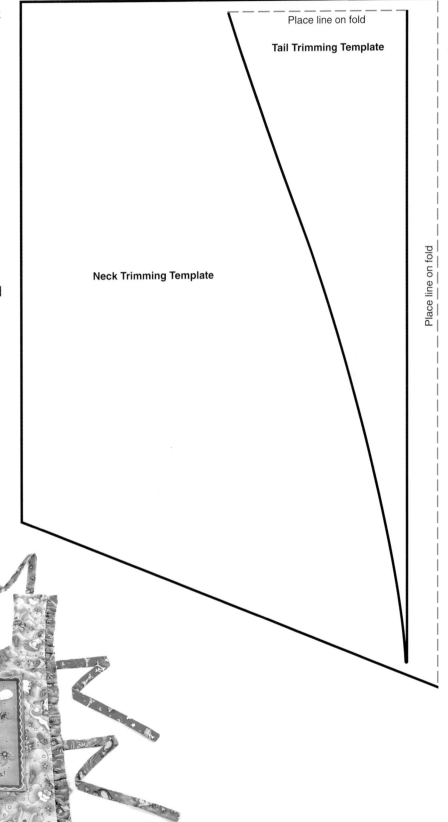

Place line on fold

Tail Trimming Template

Neck Trimming Template

Place line on fold

Quilter's Accessory Set

These quilted accessories are perfect for use when attending a quilting class.

DESIGNS BY CHRIS MALONE

PROJECT NOTE

Crushed walnut shells are a good filling for pincushions as they will sharpen the pins. They are available online and in some pet stores where they are often used on cage bottoms.

PROJECT SPECIFICATIONS

Skill Level: Intermediate
Pincushion Size: 8½" x 5½"
Needle Case Size: 4" x 8" (open)
Scissor Holder Size: 5" x 9"
Daisy Pin Size: 4¼" x 5¾"
Tulip Pin Size: 3" x 5¾"

MATERIALS FOR ALL PROJECTS

- 1 fat quarter each red, gold and green prints, and red mottled
- Needlepunched batting or thin fleece
- All-purpose thread to match fabrics
- Quilting thread (colors of choice)
- Basic sewing tools and supplies

MATERIALS FOR PINCUSHION

- 3 or 4 teaspoons crushed walnut shells (fine to medium) (optional)
- Small amount of fiberfill stuffing
- Scrap felt
- Permanent fabric adhesive

MATERIALS FOR NEEDLE CASE

- Scrap green flannel
- 5 gold glass E beads
- ½ yard ⁵⁄₁₆"-wide green grosgrain ribbon

MATERIALS FOR SCISSOR HOLDER

- ¼" gold flower bead

MATERIALS FOR FLOWER PINS

- Gold glass E beads (3 for tulip, 7 for daisy)
- Scrap felt
- Pin back for each pin
- Permanent fabric adhesive

Pincushion

Cutting

1. Prepare templates for pincushion pieces using patterns given.

2. Cut one 4"-diameter circle gold print; cut a 2"-diameter circle from batting.

3. Cut one 2"-diameter circle from felt.

Completing the Pincushion

1. Trace the pincushion petal pattern six times onto the wrong side of the red print, leaving a ½" space between shapes. Fold the fabric in half with right sides together with the traced shapes on top; pin to a piece of batting or fleece.

2. Sew all around on drawn lines, leaving the bottom edge open. Cut out each petal ⅛" from stitching lines; trim batting close to seam and clip curves.

3. Turn each petal right side out through the open end, smoothing curves; press flat.

4. Hand-quilt each petal as marked on pattern.

5. Repeat steps 1–4 with leaf pattern and green print to make two leaves.

6. To form the flower, use a knotted doubled thread to make gathering stitches along the bottom of a petal as shown in Figure 1.

Figure 1

7. Pick up a second petal and gather along the bottom onto the same thread; continue adding petals until all six are attached.

8. Stitch back into the first petal and pull the thread to gather the petals into a circle; knot and clip thread.

9. To make the flower center, center the batting circle on the wrong side of the fabric circle; hand-baste in place as shown in Figure 2.

Figure 2

10. Use a knotted doubled thread to make gathering stitches all around the edge of the fabric circle. Pull thread to gather the edges up enough to slightly cup the circle.

11. Pour crushed shells into the cupped circle and top with a small amount of fiberfill stuffing. Pull the gathering thread to close the hole, adding more fiberfill, if necessary, for a firm filling; remove

basting stitches. **Note:** *If not using crushed shells, fill the fabric circle with fiberfill; the batting circle will not be needed.*

12. To assemble the pincushion, apply permanent fabric adhesive to the bottom (gathered edges) of the flower center and press to the top of the petal circle.

13. Tuck the end of a leaf under the petals on each side; glue the base of leaves to the back of the flower.

14. Whipstitch or glue the felt circle to the bottom of the flower, covering all raw edges.

Pincushion
Placement Diagram 8½" x 5½"

Needle Case

Cutting

1. Cut one 4½" x 8½" rectangle each red mottled (A), green flannel (B) and batting or fleece.

2. Cut two 2¼" x 4½" C rectangles red print for inside pockets.

3. Cut one 1⅛" x 3" bias strip green print for stem.

4. Prepare templates for needle case pieces using patterns given. Cut petals as directed on patterns.

Completing the Needle Case

1. Fold the bias strip in half wrong sides together along length; stitch ¼" from the long raw edges. Trim seam to ⅛"; roll the tube so the seam runs down the center as shown in Figure 3 and press to make stem.

Figure 3

2. Fold A in half across width and crease to mark center. Pin the stem seam side down, to the right side of A, curving gently as shown in Figure 4; trim off excess.

Figure 4

3. Arrange the petals on A in a circle with a ½" space in the center, again referring to Figure 4.

4. To make the flower center, trace the pattern onto the wrong side of the red mottled; fold the fabric in half with right sides together and the traced circle on top. Pin to a scrap of batting or fleece. Stitch through all layers on the traced line.

5. Cut out ⅛" from the stitching line; trim batting close to seam and clip curves. Cut a slash through one layer only of the fabric. Turn the flower center right side out through the slash; press flat.

6. Appliqué the center, slash side down, to the flower, covering the petal and stem ends.

7. Place the appliquéd A right side up on top of the batting; pin or baste to hold.

8. Hand-quilt around the stem and petals.

9. Sew the glass beads to the flower center, stitching through all layers.

10. To make the inside pockets, press a double ¼" hem on one long side of each C rectangle. Topstitch along the folded edge.

11. With right sides facing up, place the hemmed C pieces at each end of B; baste ³⁄₁₆" from raw edges as shown in Figure 5.

Figure 5

12. Cut the ribbon in half and place one piece at the center of each end of B as shown in Figure 6; baste to hold in place.

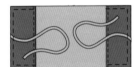

Figure 6

13. Pin the A and B panels right sides together with ribbon ends tucked inside; stitch all around, leaving a 2" opening along one long edge for turning. Trim corners; turn right side out.

14. Fold in the seam allowance on the opening; slipstitch the opening closed.

15. Fold the needle case in half; stitch on the fold line to hold the layers in place.

16. Tie a knot at each end of the ribbons; trim ends in a V to finish.

Needle Case
Placement Diagram 4" x 8" (open)

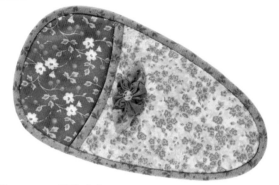

Scissor Holder

Note: *A walking foot is optional but helpful when applying the binding to the edges of the scissor holder.*

Cutting

1. Prepare templates for scissor holder front and back; cut as directed on each piece.

2. Cut a 3"-diameter circle red mottled for flower embellishment.

3. Cut a 1⅛" x 25" and a 1⅛" x 6" bias strip green print for binding, piecing as necessary with diagonal seams to make length as shown in Figure 7; press seams open.

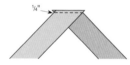

Figure 7

Completing the Holder

1. Place batting between the gold and red front holder pieces with right sides out; baste all around ³⁄₁₆" from edge. Repeat with back pieces.

2. Press one long edge of each bias strip ¼" to the wrong side.

3. Pin the long raw edge of the 6" length of binding to the top edge of the holder front layers with right side of binding against the gold side of the front; stitch in place with a scant ¼" seam allowance.

4. Trim excess binding, folding the binding over to the red lining side; hand-stitch the folded edge in place to finish top edge of front.

5. Pin the case front to the back, matching the bottom edges; baste in place as shown in Figure 8.

Figure 8

6. Starting at one side, align the raw edges of binding strip and the holder, and begin sewing 2" from the end of the strip. Sew around with a scant ¼" seam allowance. As you approach the beginning of the binding strip, stop stitching and overlap the two binding ends ½"; trim excess. Join the two ends with a ¼" seam allowance and finger-press the seam open.

7. Reposition the joined binding along the edge of the case; resume stitching to finish. Fold the binding over the back and hand-stitch the folded edge in place.

8. To make the yo-yo flower, turn in a ⅛" hem around the edge of the 3"-diameter circle; sew gathering stitches close to the folded edge, finger-pressing hem as you sew as shown in Figure 9.

Figure 9

9. Pull the stitches tightly to close the circle; smooth and flatten the yo-yo so that the hole is in the center, again referring to Figure 9. Knot the thread, but do not clip it.

10. Bring the needle over the edge of the yo-yo and back through the yo-yo center as shown in Figure 10; pull the thread to pinch the edge. Repeat on the opposite side as shown in Figure 11.

Make two more stitches to separate the circle into four equal-size petal. Using the same thread, sew a bead over the center of the flower.

| Figure 10 | Figure 11 |

11. Prepare template for leaf shape using pattern given. Trace twice onto the wrong side of the green print, leaving ½" between shapes.

12. Fold the fabric in half with right sides together and traced shapes on top. Sew all around on traced lines, leaving open at the bottom.

13. Cut out each leaf ⅛" from seam, trim tip and turn right side out. Finger-press a small pleat at the base of each leaf and tack to hold.

14. Center the yo-yo flower on the top of the front section and tuck the base of each leaf under the flower referring to the Placement Diagram for positioning; tack in place to finish scissor holder.

Scissor Holder
Placement Diagram 5" x 9"

Flower Pins

Tulip Pin

1. Prepare tulip templates using patterns given. Trace two tulip petals on the wrong side of the red print, leaving ½" between the shapes.

2. Trace one tulip petal on the wrong side of the red mottled.

3. Fold the fabrics in half with right sides together with traced shapes on top; pin to a piece of batting or fleece.

4. Sew all around on the drawn lines; cut out each petal ⅛" from the stitching line; trim the batting close to the seam. Trim tips and clip curves.

5. Cut a slash on one edge of each petal through one layer only as shown in Figure 12. ***Note:** Be sure that the slash is on the wrong side of the print petals.*

Figure 12

6. Turn each petal right side out through the slash; press flat. Whipstitch the cut edges together. ***Note:** The slashes will be covered when the flower is assembled. The right side of the center petal is the side with the slash; the outer petals will have the slash on the back side.*

7. Hand-quilt a double line around each petal.

8. Repeat steps 1–6 to make a leaf and stem with green tonal, leaving the top edge of the stem piece open and trimming the stitched end as close as possible to the seam without weakening the seam.

9. Hand-quilt ¼" from edge and along the center of leaf.

10. Carefully turn the stem right side out through the open end. *Note: A firm narrow tool with a rounded end, such as a small crochet hook, is helpful in pushing the stem through.* Press seam; hand-quilt a line down the center.

11. To assemble the flower, place the top of the stem over the bottom of the right side (slash side) of the center petal about ⅜"; tack or glue to secure.

12. Arrange the two outer petals on each side so the slash lines are against the center petal and the edges overlap slightly in the center; tack or glue in place.

13. Tack or glue the leaf to the stem with the slash against the stem.

14. Sew three beads to the center petal where the outer petals meet.

15. Sew a pin back to the back side of the center petal to finish.

Daisy Pin

1. Prepare templates for daisy pieces using patterns given.

2. Trace the daisy petal five times on the wrong side of the gold print, leaving ½" between the shapes.

3. Fold the fabric in half, right sides together, with traced shape on top, and pin to a piece of batting or fleece.

4. Sew all around, leaving open at the bottom. Cut out each petal ⅛" from the stitching line; trim batting close to seam. Clip curves and turn right side out; press flat.

5. Hand-quilt a double line of stitches around each petal.

6. Repeat steps 2–4 with the flower center and red mottled, except cut a slash on the wrong side through one layer only and turn right side out through the slash. Whipstitch the cut edges together and press flat.

7. Sew seven beads to the flower center referring to the Placement Diagram for positioning.

8. Make one stem and one leaf referring to steps 8–10 for the Tulip Pin.

9. Cut a 1½" circle from felt.

10. To assemble the daisy, place the top of the stem over the edge of the felt circle about ⅜"; tack or glue to secure.

11. Arrange the five petals evenly around the outer edge of the felt circle as shown in Figure 13; tack or glue in place.

Figure 13

12. Cover the petal ends with the flower center; tack or glue in place.

13. Tack or glue the leaf to the stem with the slash against the stem.

14. Sew a pin back to the back side of the felt circle to finish. ◆

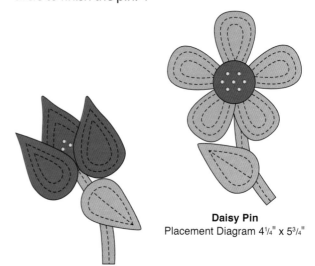

Daisy Pin
Placement Diagram 4¼" x 5¾"

Tulip Pin
Placement Diagram 3" x 5¾"

Scissor Holder Front
Cut 1 each red & gold prints
& 1 batting

Needle Case Petal 3
Cut 2 gold print
(reverse 1)

Pincushion Petal
Cut as directed

Daisy Petal
Cut as
directed

Tulip Petal
Cut as directed

Stem
Cut as directed

Scissor Holder Back
Cut 1 each red & gold prints
& 1 batting

Scissor Holder Leaf
Cut as directed

Flower Pin Leaf
Cut as directed

Daisy Center & Back
Cut as directed

**Needle Case
Center**

**Needle Case
Petal 1**
Cut 1 gold print

Pincushion Leaf
Cut as directed

**Needle Case
Petal 2**
Cut 2 gold print
(reverse 1)

Baby Bibs Twins

Whether the new baby in your life is a boy or a girl, he or she will look perfect in this bib duo.

DESIGN BY LORINE MASON

PROJECT SPECIFICATIONS

Skill Level: Beginner
Bib Size: 8" x 7½"

MATERIALS

- 5 coordinating pastel fat quarters
- Batting 10" x 10" for each bib
- All-purpose thread to match fabrics
- 1 package extra-wide double-fold bias tape to coordinate with fabrics
- 1 yard picot trim
- 1 (½") aqua button
- 4 (⅝") pink buttons
- Basic sewing tools and supplies

Cutting

1. Prepare pattern for the bib; cut one piece of batting for each bib, cutting batting at least 1" larger than the shape all around. Mark a centerline from side to side on a batting shape for a boy bib or from top to bottom for a girl bib.

2. Using the pattern, cut one backing piece for each bib from any fat quarter.

3. Prepare tie template; cut as directed.

4. Cut a 1¾" x 21" strip from each fat quarter.

5. Cut a 1" x 7" strip from one fat quarter for button placket.

Completing the It's a Boy Bib

1. Place one 1¾"-wide strip on the boy bib batting shape along the marked centerline; place a second strip on top. Stitch and press strip to the right side as shown in Figure 1; trim strips even with batting.

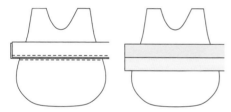

Figure 1

2. Repeat step 1 until batting piece is covered.

3. Lay the bib pattern on the patchwork top; trace around outside edges. Stitch along the edges of the traced lines.

4. Cut out the bib close to the outside edge of the stitched lines.

5. Pin the tie pieces right sides together; stitch around, leaving the top narrow edge open. Trim point and turn right side out; press flat.

6. Center and pin the tie piece with narrow end even with neck edge; baste to hold.

7. Stitch tie in place ⅛" from edge through all layers.

8. Place a bib backing piece with the wrong side against the batting side of the stitched unit and pin to hold layers together.

9. Referring to Figure 2, enclose outside edges of bib with bias binding and topstitch through all layers using a decorative stitch such as a blanket stitch.

Figure 2

10. Cut a 30" length of bias binding for neck edge; center the strip on the neck edge and stitch in place as in step 8.

11. Sew a button to the center of the tie to finish.

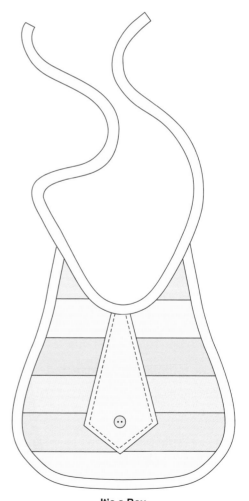

It's a Boy
Placement Diagram 8" x 7½"

Completing the It's a Girl Bib

1. Cut an odd-shaped piece no larger than 3" from any one of the fat quarters. ***Note:*** *A five-sided shape is ideal; a pattern has been provided should you want to use it.*

2. Lay the piece right side up on the girl batting shape, placing slightly off-center; pin to hold.

3. Cut a second piece of fabric at least as long as one of the sides of the first patch plus ½"; lay this patch right sides together on top of the first patch, aligning the raw edges; pin and then stitch along raw edges as shown in Figure 3. Press the second piece to the right side and pin flat referring to Figure 4.

Figure 3   **Figure 4**

4. Continue adding pieces in this manner, working in a clockwise direction, until the batting is covered.

5. Using a variety of decorative stitches, stitch along the seams between pieces.

6. Lay the bib pattern on the patchwork top; trace around outside edges. Stitch along the edges of the traced lines.

7. Cut out the bib close to the outside edge of the stitched lines.

8. Turn under ¼" along each long side of the 1" x 7" button placket strip; press.

9. Center and pin the strip down the front of the bib. Insert and pin a 7" length of picot trim under each long side of the center strip as shown in Figure 5.

Figure 5

10. Topstitch down each side of the strip through all layers as shown in Figure 6; trim strip even with bib edges.

Figure 6

11. Pin and baste an 8" length of picot trim along the curved neck area; trim to fit.

12. Place a bib backing piece with the wrong side against the batting side of the stitched unit and pin to hold layers together.

13. Bind edges as in steps 8 and 9 in Completing the It's a Boy Bib.

14. Evenly space and sew four buttons to the center front of the bib to finish. ◆

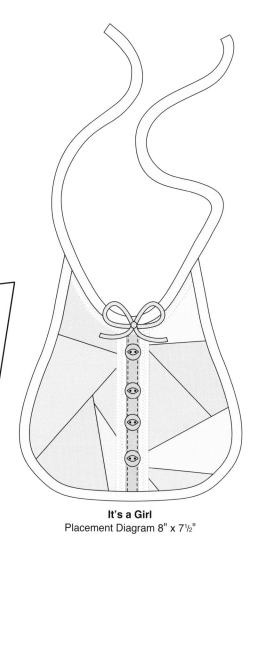

It's a Girl
Placement Diagram 8" x 7½"

Optional 5-Sided Template

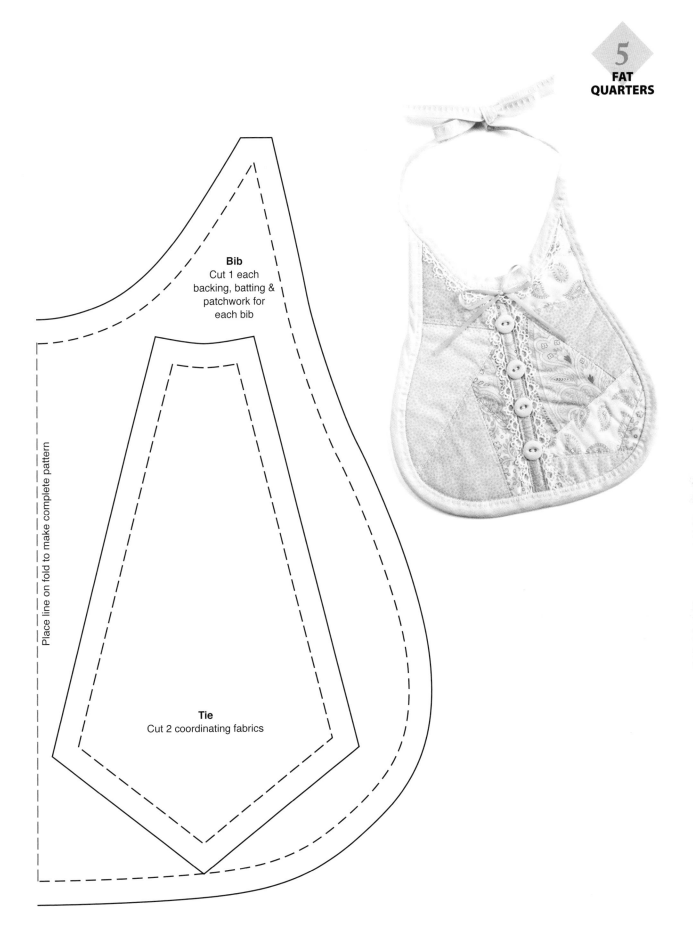

Bib
Cut 1 each
backing, batting &
patchwork for
each bib

Place line on fold to make complete pattern

Tie
Cut 2 coordinating fabrics

Fat-Quarter Tote

This large tote is perfect for shopping trips to your favorite quilt shop.

DESIGN BY LORINE MASON

PROJECT SPECIFICATIONS

Skill Level: Beginner
Tote Size: 13" x 17" x 4"

MATERIALS

- 5 coordinating fat quarters
- 2 (18" x 24") pieces lightweight cotton batting
- Neutral-color all-purpose thread
- 1¼ yards coordinating cotton strapping
- 5 (1½") white buttons
- Basic sewing tools and supplies

Cutting

1. Cut two 2½" x 21" A strips from each of the five fat quarters.

2. Cut two 4¼" x 21" B strips from two of the fat quarters.

3. Cut one 2" x 12" C strip from one of the B-strip fat quarters and a 3" x 12" D strip from the other.

4. Cut two of the remaining three fat quarters in half along the 21" length to make four 6½" x 21" E strips.

5. Cut the remaining fat quarter into four 3¼" x 21" F strips.

Completing the Tote

1. Lay one of the 18" x 24" batting pieces on a flat surface; pin one of the B strips right side up on the batting, aligning left side edges. Stitch ¼" in from the left edge down the length of the strip.

2. Lay one A strip right sides together on top of the right side edge of the B strip; pin through all layers of fabric and batting. Stitch along long edge using a ¼" seam; press A away from B and toward the center as shown in Figure 1.

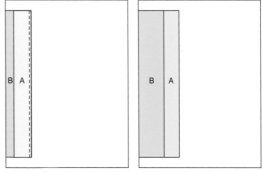

Figure 1

3. Continue sewing and pressing four more A strips and one B strip to the batting in the same manner, ending with a B strip as shown in Figure 2. Trim the finished piece to measure 18" x 21" to complete the bag front; set aside.

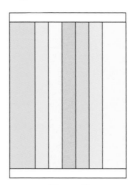

Figure 2

4. Repeat steps 1–3 to create the bag back.

5. Stitch a C strip to a D strip along the 12" edges; press seam to one side.

6. Fold the C-D strip in half with right sides together to make a 4½" x 6" pocket unit as shown in Figure 3; stitch across the top and side edges, leaving the bottom edge open, again referring to Figure 3.

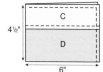

Figure 3

7. Turn the pocket unit right side out; press flat.

8. Center and hand-stitch a button on the seam line of the pocket front as shown in Figure 4.

Figure 4

9. Center and pin the pocket right sides together with the top edge 3" from the bottom seam of the bag front as shown in Figure 5; stitch across the bottom raw edge, again referring to Figure 5.

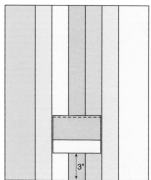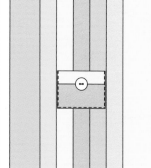

Figure 5

10. Press the pocket up; pin and topstitch around sides and across the bottom to hold in place, again referring to Figure 5.

11. Pin and stitch the bag front and back pieces right sides together along sides and across bottom using a ½" seam allowance.

12. Align side seams with bottom seams, spreading bottom corner to make a triangle as shown in Figure 6; stitch from fold to fold 2" from point to complete square corners as shown in Figure 6.

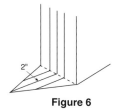

Figure 6

13. Join the E and F strips, alternating strips as shown in Figure 7; press seams to one side.

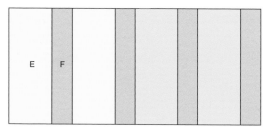

Figure 7

14. Measure and trim width to measure 35", trimming an equal amount off each end as shown in Figure 8.

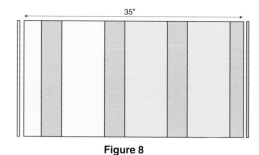

Figure 8

15. Join the E-F unit on the short ends using a ½" seam allowance, and then along one layered raw edge to complete the bag lining as shown in Figure 9; press seams open.

Figure 9

16. Repeat step 12 to make bottom corners.

17. Insert the lining into the bag with wrong sides together, matching seams and corners; pin top edges together.

18. Roll the batting and lining of the bag over the top to the outside 1½" as shown in Figure 10; press. Repeat, rolling both layers over another 1½" to the front, again referring to Figure 10; topstitch through all layers ½" from top edge.

Figure 10

19. Press the seam to the inside of the bag 1" down from the top edge as shown in Figure 11.

Figure 11

20. Cut the strapping piece in half to make two equal lengths. Fold each end under 1". Pin ends to the front and back of the bag 2" from top edge and 4" in from side edges as shown in Figure 12; stitch through all layers as shown in Figure 13.

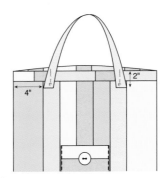

Figure 12

Figure 13

21. Sew a button onto the folded strap ends to finish. ◆

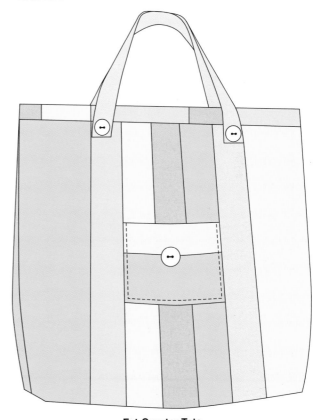

Fat-Quarter Tote
Placement Diagram 13" x 17" x 4"

Cone Flower Wall Hanging

Use the beauty of batiks to create this wall quilt which celebrates nature with the simple coneflower and autumn leaves.

DESIGN BY CAROLYN S. VAGTS

PROJECT SPECIFICATIONS

Skill Level: Advanced
Wall Hanging Size: 31" x 35"

MATERIALS

- 1 fat quarter tan batik (S)
- 1 batik fat quarter each medium pink (N), medium plum (O), medium-dark plum (P) and dark plum (R)
- Gold, green and lavender/green batik scraps for appliqué
- ¾ yard light multicolored batik
- ⅞ yard brown/rust batik
- Backing 39" x 43"
- Batting 39" x 43"
- All-purpose thread to match fabrics
- Quilting thread
- 1 yard 15"-wide fusible web
- Basic sewing tools and supplies

Cutting

1. Cut one of each of the following from light multicolored batik for background pieces: 5½" x 5½" B, 4½" x 6½" C, 4½" x 4½" D, 3½" x 6½" E, 3½" x 7½" F, 4½" x 5½ H and 9½" x 13½" I.

2. Cut two 3½" x 4½" G and four 4½" x 8½" A pieces light multicolored batik for background pieces.

3. Cut one 3½" x 6½" J rectangle from medium pink batik fat quarter.

4. Cut three 1½" x 21" strips from each N, O, P, R, and S fat quarter. *Note: These strips will be stitched to the units, pressed and then trimmed to*

size during construction. Cut additional strips as needed during piecing.

5. Cut two 2½" by fabric width strips brown/rust batik; subcut strips into two 5½" K, two 11½" L and two 19½" M strips.

6. Cut two 1½" by fabric width Q strips brown/rust batik.

7. Cut two 2½" x 27½" T strips and two 2½" x 35½" U strips brown/rust batik.

8. Cut four 2¼" by fabric width strips brown/rust batik for binding.

Completing the Appliqué

1. Trace leaf and flower appliqué shapes onto the paper side of the fusible web as directed on patterns for number to cut, leaving a margin between pieces; cut out shapes, leaving a margin around each one.

2. Fuse shapes to the wrong side of fabrics as directed on patterns for color; cut out shapes on traced lines. Remove paper backing.

3. Referring to Figure 1, fuse shapes to background pieces, layering motifs in numerical order referring to patterns.

4. When fusing is complete, straight-stitch close to the edge around each motif using thread to match fabrics.

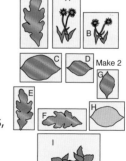

Figure 1

5. Add flower details using a straight stitch referring to patterns for positioning.

Completing the Top

1. Select an R strip; sew to the top of the appliquéd I block. Trim end of strip even with I and press strip to the right side as shown in Figure 2.

Figure 2

2. Repeat step 1 with R on the bottom of I; press seams toward R. Repeat on the long sides of I.

3. Sew an L strip to the top and bottom of the I unit, sew M strips to opposite long sides and add an N strip to the bottom to complete the 15½" x 20½" large flower (I) section as shown in Figure 3.

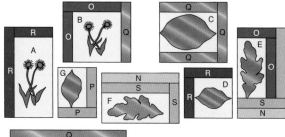

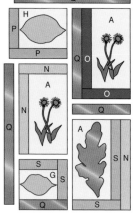

Figure 3

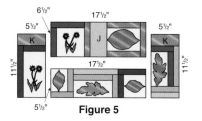

Figure 5

4. In the same manner, sew the N–S strips to the appliquéd A–H pieces, again referring to Figure 3 for positioning of strips.

5. Join three A units and one each G and H units as shown in Figure 4 to make the 12½" x 20½" lower left section; press. Sew the lower left section to the large flower (I) section to complete the bottom section, again referring to Figure 4; press seam toward the large flower (I) section.

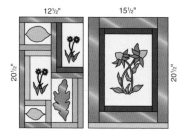

Figure 4

6. Join one each A–G units with J and K pieces to make one each 5½" x 11½" left, 17½" x 6½" upper, 17½" x 5½" lower and 5½" x 11½" right sections; press. Join the sections to complete the top section, again referring to Figure 5; press.

7. Join the top and bottom sections to complete the pieced center; press seam toward the bottom section.

8. Sew a T strip to the top and bottom and U strips to opposite long sides to complete the top; press seams toward T and U strips.

Completing the Wall Hanging

1. Sandwich batting between the pieced top and prepared backing; pin or baste layers together.

2. Quilt as desired by hand or machine. When quilting is complete, remove pins or basting and trim excess backing and batting even with runner edges.

3. Join binding strips on short ends with diagonal seams to make one long strip; trim seams to ¼" and press open.

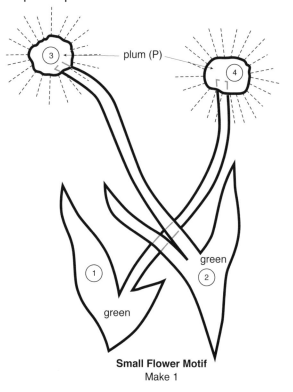

Small Flower Motif
Make 1

4. Fold and press the binding strip with wrong sides together along length to make a double-layered binding strip.

5. Sew binding to the right side of the wall hanging with raw edges even, mitering corners and overlapping ends; press binding away from the edges and turn to the back side. Hand- or machine-stitch in place to finish. ◆

Cone Flower Wall Hanging
Placement Diagram 31" x 35"

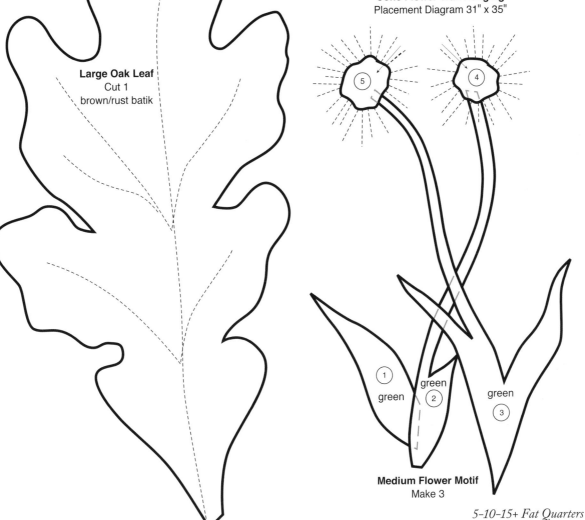

Large Oak Leaf
Cut 1
brown/rust batik

Medium Flower Motif
Make 3

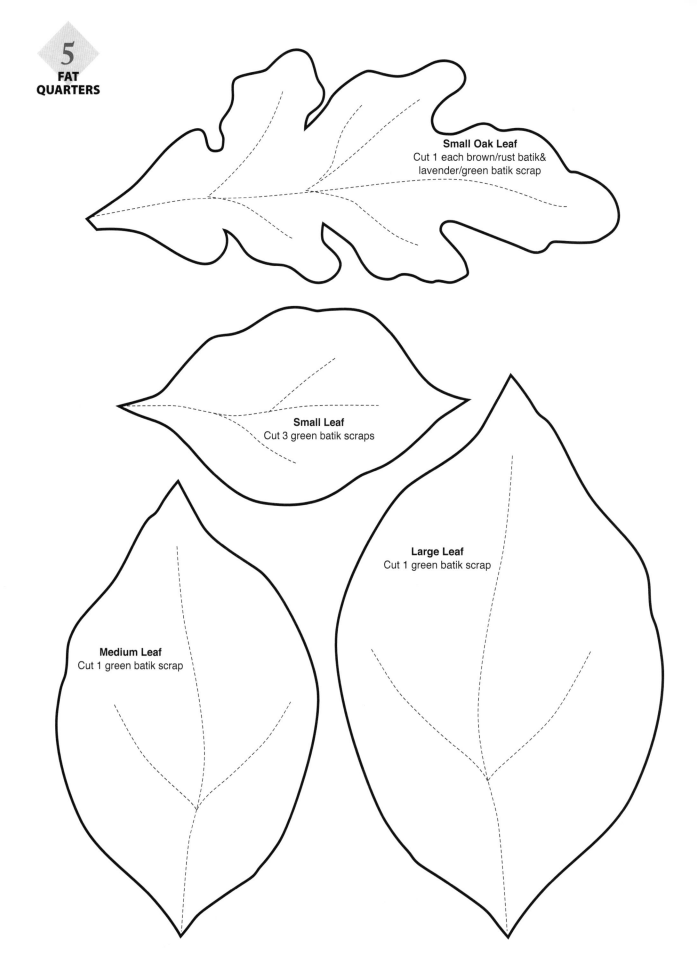

Small Oak Leaf
Cut 1 each brown/rust batik&
lavender/green batik scrap

Small Leaf
Cut 3 green batik scraps

Large Leaf
Cut 1 green batik scrap

Medium Leaf
Cut 1 green batik scrap

Large Flower Motif
Make 1

Big Bead Bag

A magnetic snap makes this purse practical, and the oversized beads make it fun and fabulous!

DESIGNS BY LYNN SCHIEFELBEIN FROM OAK STREET QUILTERS

PROJECT SPECIFICATIONS

Skill Level: Beginner
Bag Size: 17½" x 17½" x 7"

MATERIALS

- 5 coordinating fat quarters
- 1¼ yards lining
- All-purpose thread to match fabrics
- 1¼ yards 22"-wide lightweight fusible interfacing
- 26 (1") wooden beads
- 1 magnetic snap set
- 4"-long needle
- Basic sewing tools and supplies

Cutting

1. Assign a letter (A–E) to each fat quarter. Cut two 4" x 18" A strips and four each 4" x 18" B and C strips from fat quarters. Cut two each 4" x 18" D and E strips from fat quarters.

2. Cut one 7½" x 18" F strip from the D fat quarter.

3. Cut one 4" x 21" G strip for handle from the D fat quarter.

4. Cut two 2" x 21" H strips for handle from the A fat quarter.

5. Cut one 25" x 42½" lining rectangle.

6. Cut two 18" x 18", three 7½" x 18", one 2" x 22" and one 1" x 22" pieces of lightweight fusible interfacing.

Completing the Bag

1. Join one A strip and two each B and C strips with right sides together along length to make an A-B-C panel as shown in Figure 1; press seams in one direction. Repeat to make a second panel.

Figure 1

2. Fuse one 18" x 18" square interfacing to the wrong side of each A-B-C panel.

3. Join one each D and E strip with right sides together along length; press seam to one side. Repeat to make two D-E strips.

4. Fuse one 7½" x 18" piece of interfacing to the wrong side of each D-E strip.

5. Sew a D-E strip to one edge of each A-B-C panel, stopping stitching ¼" from bottom edge as shown in Figure 2; backstitch to secure seams. Press seams to one side.

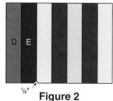

¼" **Figure 2**

6. Fuse the 7½" x 18" piece of interfacing to the wrong side of F.

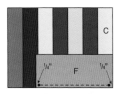
7. Sew F to the bottom edge of the front panel with one end of F aligned with the C end of the panel, starting and stopping stitching ¼" from each end of F as shown in Figure 3.

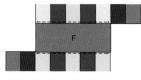

Figure 3   Figure 4

8. Repeat step 7 on the bottom edge of the second panel, aligning the C end of the panel with the end of F opposite the end aligned with the front panel as shown in Figure 4.

9. Press seam allowances toward the front and back panels; topstitch close to seams again referring to Figure 4.

10. Join the D-E strips to the opposite C strips on panels, stopping stitching ¼" from bottom edge as shown in Figure 5 to make bag ends.

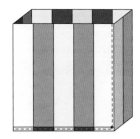

Figure 5   Figure 6

11. Join bottom edge of strips to the short ends of F, starting and stopping ¼" from ends to make a square bottom as shown in Figure 6.

12. Center and fuse the 2" x 22" interfacing strip to the wrong side of the G strip; fold outer edges of G to the center of the wrong side of the strip as shown in Figure 7 and press.

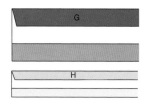

Figure 7

13. Center and fuse the 1" x 22" interfacing strip to the wrong side of the H strip; fold outer edges of H to the center of the wrong side of the strip and press, again referring to Figure 7.

14. Center the H strip on the folded side of the G strip, covering the raw edges of G to make a reversible handle as shown in Figure 8; topstitch close to the edges of H to hold in place.

Figure 8

Big Bead Bag
Placement Diagram 17½" x 17½" x 7"

15. Fold the lining piece in half with right sides together to make a 25" x 21¼" rectangle; sew short edges together, leaving a 4½" opening on one side as shown in Figure 9.

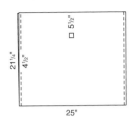

Figure 9

16. Measure 5½" from the center of the long open end on the front and back of the lining and mark. Add a small square of lightweight fusible interfacing to the wrong side of each side to cover the marked spot, again referring to Figure 9.

17. Add a magnetic snap to the right side of the front and back of the lining on the marked spot referring to the instructions with the snap set.

18. Mark a curved cutting line on each top edge on the wrong side of the lining, beginning at the side seams and dropping by 2¼" at the center of each side as shown in Figure 10.

Figure 10   **Figure 11**

19. Center one side seam of the lining over the center fold of the bottom, right sides together as shown in Figure 11. Measure and mark a sewing line across the folded point and up 3¾" from the point; sew along marked line to make a square corner, again referring to Figure 11. Trim seam to ¼" and press.

20. Center and baste the G-H handle strip on each D-E top edge of the outer bag as shown in Figure 12. Repeat on the opposite side.

Figure 12

21. Insert bag inside lining with right sides together, matching side seams.

22. Sew ¼" from the marked curved line through both layers as shown in Figure 13.

Figure 13

23. Trim excess from the curved stitching line, leaving a ¼" seam allowance; turn right side out through opening in lining. Press along top edge to keep lining inside; topstitch close to edge. Turn in opening edges in lining to the inside and stitch lining opening closed.

Figure 14

24. Pinch-fold 1" on the top edge at each seam between the strips and in the center of each strip as shown in Figure 14 and, using the 4" needle with 2 strands of thread, attach the beads by sewing through the pinched folds and then through a bead. Continue across, adding a bead between each pinched fold, using nine each on the front and back, and four on each end to finish. ◆

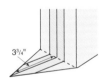

Warm Breeze Runner

Entertain your friends in style with this warm and winsome runner decorating your table.

DESIGN BY PHYLLIS DOBBS

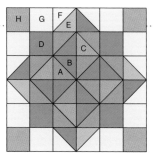

Warm Breeze
13½" x 13½" Block
Make 3

PROJECT SPECIFICATIONS

Skill Level: Beginner
Runner Size: 60" x 15½"
Block Size: 13½" x 13½"
Number of Blocks: 3

MATERIALS

- 1 fat quarter medium blue tonal
- 1 fat quarter tan tonal
- 1 fat quarter blue print
- 1 fat quarter green print
- 1 fat quarter green checkerboard
- 1 fat quarter rust print
- ¼ yard medium blue tonal
- ½ yard coordinating stripe
- Backing 68" x 24"
- Batting 68" x 24"
- Multicolored cotton thread
- Quilting thread
- Basic sewing tools and supplies

Cutting

1. Cut three 3⅛" x 21" strips blue print; subcut strips into (18) 3⅛" A squares.

2. Cut one 7⅝" x 21" strip blue print; subcut strip into one 7⅝" K square.

3. Cut three 3⅛" x 21" strips green print; subcut strips into (18) 3⅛" B squares.

4. Cut two 2¾" x 21" strips green print; subcut strips into (12) 2¾" D squares.

5. Cut one 3⅛" x 21" strip rust print; subcut strip into six 3⅛" C squares.

6. Cut one 7⅝" x 21" strip rust print; subcut strip into two 7⅝" J squares.

7. Cut two 2¾" x 21" strips rust print; subcut strips into (12) 2¾" H squares.

8. Cut one 3⅛" x 21" strip green checkerboard; subcut strip into six 3⅛" E squares.

9. Cut one 7⅝" x 21" strip green checkerboard; subcut strip into one 7⅝" L square.

10. Cut two 3⅛" x 21" strips tan tonal; subcut strip into (12) 3⅛" F squares.

11. Cut four 2¾" x 21" strips tan tonal; subcut strips into (24) 2¾" G squares.

12. Cut one 2½" by fabric width strip coordinating stripe; subcut strip into two 14" I strips.

13. Cut four 2¼" by fabric width strips coordinating stripe for binding.

14. Cut one 1½" by fabric width strip of medium blue tonal; subcut strip into two 14" M strips.

15. Cut three 1½" by fabric width N strips medium blue tonal.

Completing the Blocks

1. Draw a diagonal line from corner to corner on the wrong side of each A and F square.

2. Pair an A square with a B square right sides together; stitch ¼" on each side of the marked line as shown in Figure 1. Cut apart on the marked line to make two A-B units, again referring to Figure 1. Repeat to make a total of 24 A-B units.

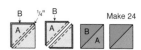

Figure 1   **Figure 2**

3. Repeat step 2 with A and C to make 12 A-C units, with E and F to make 12 E-F units, and with B and F to make 12 B-F units referring to Figure 2.

4. To make one Warm Breeze block, select eight A-B units and four each A-C, E-F and B-F units, four each D and H squares, and eight G squares.

5. Referring to Figure 3, join two A-B units to make a row; repeat. Press seams in opposite directions. Join the two rows to make the center pinwheel unit; press seam to one side.

Figure 3   **Figure 4**   **Figure 5**

6. Sew an A-B unit to an A-C unit as shown in Figure 4; press seam to one side. Sew an E-F unit to a B-F unit, again referring to Figure 4; press seam to one side. Join the two rows to complete one side unit; press seam to one side. Repeat to make four side units.

7. Referring to Figure 5, join one each D and H square, and two G squares to complete a corner unit; press seams in rows in opposite directions. Repeat to make four corner units.

8. Sew a side unit to opposite sides of the pinwheel center to make the center row as shown in Figure 6; press seams away from the side units.

9. Sew a corner unit to opposite sides of each remaining side unit to make the top and bottom rows, again referring to Figure 6; press seams toward corner units.

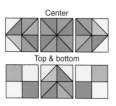
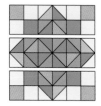

Figure 6   **Figure 7**

10. Join the rows referring to Figure 7 to complete one Warm Breeze block; press seams in one direction.

11. Repeat Steps 4–10 to complete three Warm Breeze blocks.

Completing the Runner

1. Join the three Warm Breeze blocks to make the pieced center; press seams in one direction.

2. Sew an I strip to each end of the pieced center; press seams toward I strips.

3. Draw a diagonal line from corner to corner on the wrong side of each J square.

4. Place a J square right sides together with K and one with L; stitch ¼" on each side of the marked lines. Cut each stitched unit apart on the marked line to make two each J-K and J-L units as in step 2 and Figure 1 for Completing the Blocks.

5. Join one each J-K and J-L units to make two end units as shown in Figure 8; press seams to one side.

Figure 8

Continued on page 170

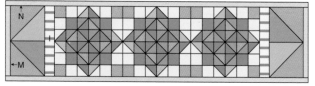

Warm Breeze Runner
Placement Diagram 60" x 15½"

Americana Checkerboard

Make a fabric checkerboard and matching storage bag in navy, red and cream fabrics for an Americana look.

DESIGN BY JODI G. WARNER

PROJECT SPECIFICATIONS

Skill Level: Intermediate
Board Size: 31½" x 31½"
Bag Size: Approximately 7" x 18"

MATERIALS

- 1 fat quarter navy/cream stripe
- 1 fat quarter red/cream stripe
- 2 fat quarters navy/cream star prints
- 2 fat quarters cream prints
- ½ yard red print
- 1 yard blue print
- Backing 37" x 37"
- Thin batting 37" x 37"
- All-purpose thread to match fabrics
- 24 wooden 2⅜" diameter checker disks
- Red and blue acrylic paint
- Glazing medium (optional)
- Dark brown stencil cream (optional)
- Acrylic protective spray (optional)
- Blank stencil plastic (optional)
- Stencil brush (optional)
- ⅝ yard narrow red poly cord
- 1 cord stop
- Basic sewing tools and supplies

Checkerboard

Cutting

1. Cut three 3½" x 21" A strips from each navy star fat quarter.

2. Cut three 3½" x 21" B strips from each cream fat quarter.

3. Cut two 1¼" x 12½" C strips each red/cream and navy/cream stripes.

4. Cut two 1¼" x 13¼" D strips each red/cream and navy/cream stripes.

5. Cut two 3½" x 13¼" E strips each red and blue prints.

6. Cut two 3½" x 16¼" F strips each red and blue prints.

7. Cut two 2¼" by fabric width strips each red and blue prints.

Completing the Checkerboard

1. Sew an A strip to a B strip with right sides together along length; press seams toward A strips. Repeat to make six strip sets.

2. Subcut the A-B strip sets into (32) 3½" A-B units as shown in Figure 1.

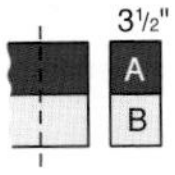

3½"

Figure 1

3. Join four A-B units to make a row as shown in Figure 2; press seams toward A. Repeat to make eight rows.

Figure 2

4. Join the rows, turning every other row as shown in Figure 3; press seams in one direction.

Figure 3

5. Join one red C and one navy C on the short ends to make a C border strip; press seam to one side. Repeat to make two C border strips.

6. Sew a C border strip to opposite sides of the pieced center referring to the Placement Diagram for positioning of colors; press seams toward C border strips.

7. Repeat steps 5 and 6 red and navy D strips to make D border strips.

8. Sew D border strips to the top and bottom of the pieced center; press seams toward D border strips.

9. Repeat steps 5 and 6 with red and blue E strips to make E border strips.

10. Sew E border strips to opposite sides of the pieced center; press seams toward E border strips.

11. Repeat steps 5 and 6 with red and blue F strips to make F border strips.

12. Sew F border strips to the top and bottom of the pieced center; press seams toward F border strips to complete the pieced top.

13. Sandwich batting between the completed top and prepared backing; pin or baste layers together to hold flat.

14. Quilt as desired by hand or machine.

15. When quilting is complete, remove pins or basting and trim edges even.

16. Fold each binding strip in half along length with wrong sides together and press.

17. Place a blue binding strip on the right side of the pieced top at the seam between the blue and red border strips as shown in Figure 4, leaving a 4" tail extending onto the red border.

Figure 4

18. Sew binding strip to the pieced top beginning 3" from the blue/red border seam, mitering corner, stopping 3" from the blue/red border seam and leaving the remainder of the strip loose on the adjacent side as shown in Figure 5.

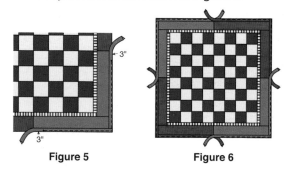

Figure 5   Figure 6

19. Repeat steps 17 and 18 with the remaining binding strips, sewing red binding to the red edges and blue binding to the remaining blue edges and leaving ends loose as shown in Figure 6.

20. Unfold the loose ends of binding strips; fold these loose ends and crease at the exact spot that the strips will meet the blue/red border seam as shown in Figure 7. Trim excess from binding strips ¼" from creases.

21. Join the binding strip ends with a straight seam to meet exactly at the center seams on each side of the top, again referring to Figure 7; press seams open.

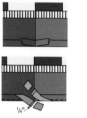
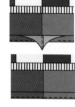

| Figure 7 | Figure 8 |

22. Refold the joined binding strip in half; stitch to the edges of the quilted top, with binding and border seams matching as shown in Figure 8.

23. Press binding away from the quilt edges and turn to the back side; hand- or machine-stitch binding in place to finish.

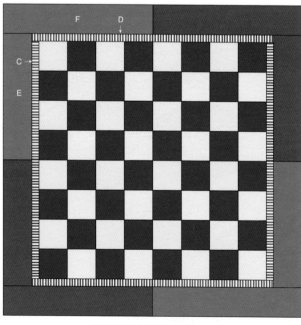

Americana Checkerboard
Placement Diagram 31½" x 31½"

Storage Bag

Cutting

1. Cut one 15" x 18¾" G piece blue print.

2. Cut one 15" x 12¾" H piece blue print for lining.

3. Cut one 9½" x 15" I strip navy/cream stripe for bag upper lining/casing.

Completing the Bag

1. Sew I between G and H as shown in Figure 9; press seams toward G and H. Measure 1½" from the G/I seam and fold the pieced unit with wrong sides together as shown in Figure 10. Press to make a sharp crease; unfold.

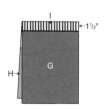

| Figure 9 | Figure 10 |

2. Fold the unit along length with right sides together; press to create side crease as shown in Figure 11. Make a mark ⅜" below G/I seam for casing, again referring to Figure 11.

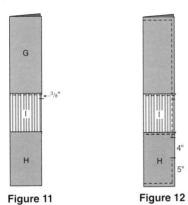

Figure 11   **Figure 12**

3. Stitch a ½" seam allowance, locking stitches at each side of casing opening and leaving a 4" opening for turning 5" from bottom ends referring to Figure 12; stitch across each end, again referring to Figure 12; press seams open.

4. At each end of the bag, reposition to match bottom seam with side crease or seam at each corner; pin. Measure and mark a line 1¾" from point, perpendicular to end seam. Stitch across marked line, securing stitches at each end. Trim excess, leaving a ¼" seam allowance referring to Figure 13.

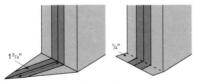

Figure 13

5. Turn the stitched unit right side out through opening; press crease at end seams and between ends of seams to form a boxed base. Turn in seam allowance at opening; hand-stitch opening closed.

6. Insert lining into body, arranging crease in I piece to be the top of the bag. Topstitch through both layers along the seam between the I and G

pieces and ⅜" from the G piece to form the casing as shown in Figure 14.

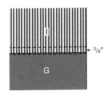

Figure 14

7. Insert cord through casing. Attach cord stops and knot ends.

8. To store checkers and mat, fold mat in quarters and then roll tightly and insert into bag along with checkers.

Making Checkers

1. Prepare optional star stencil using blank stencil plastic and pattern given.

2. Paint 12 each red and blue checkers, mixing paint with glazing medium for a more transparent finish.

3. Stencil a brown star onto one side only of each checker.

4. Antique checkers with stain and finish with acrylic protective spray. ◆

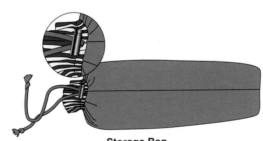

Storage Bag
Placement Diagram 7" x 18"

Star Design
Paint one design on each wooden circle as instructed

Bags in Blue

We made our bag and matching coin purse using seven fat quarters in blue. Select fat quarters in your favorite colors to make your bags. You'll love using them!

DESIGNS BY CAROLYN S. VAGTS

PROJECT SPECIFICATIONS

Skill Level: Beginner
Purse Size: Approximately 16" x 12½"
Coin Purse Size: 9½" x 7½"

MATERIALS

- 7 coordinating fat quarters
- ½ yard lining fabric
- ½ yard dark solid
- ½ yard fusible batting
- Backing 42" x 42"
- All-purpose thread to match fabrics
- 7" zipper to match fabrics
- 1 (1¾") round designer button
- Basic sewing tools and supplies

Cutting

1. Cut one 2½" x 20" A strip from each of the seven fat quarters and the dark solid.

2. Cut one each 2½" x 10" F strip from four fat quarters and the dark solid.

3. Select one of the fat quarters to cut one 12" x 20" B pocket rectangle.

4. Cut one 3½" by fabric width strip from the dark solid; subcut strip into four 3½" x 10½" C strips.

5. Cut two 4" x 27" D strips dark solid for handles.

6. Cut one 1¼" x 5" E strip dark solid for purse closure loop.

7. Cut one 1½" x 6" G strip dark solid for coin purse loop.

8. Cut one 16½" x 20" purse lining rectangle from lining fabric.

9. Cut one 8" x 10" coin purse lining from lining fabric.

10. Cut one 16½" x 20" rectangle fusible batting for purse body.

11. Cut two 3½" x 10½" strips fusible batting for purse top band.

12. Cut two 2" x 27" strips fusible batting for handles.

13. Cut one 8" x 10" rectangle fusible batting for coin purse.

Completing the Purse

1. Arrange and join the A strips in a pleasing order with right sides together along the 20" sides to make an A panel; press seams in one direction.

2. Fuse the A panel to the 16½" x 20" rectangle fusible batting with fusible side of batting against the wrong side of the A panel.

3. Fold the 12" x 20" B rectangle in half with right sides together to make a 6" x 20" rectangle; stitch along the long raw edge as shown in Figure 1. Turn right side out; press edges flat with seam at bottom.

Figure 1

4. Measure and mark down 2½" from the top edge of the 16½" x 20" lining rectangle; pin the pocket to the right side of the lining with the top folded edge even with the 2½" mark and raw edges aligned as shown in Figure 2.

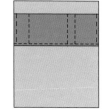

Figure 2   Figure 3

5. Baste in place at side edges and stitch across bottom stitched end; divide and stitch the pocket into sections as desired referring to Figure 3.

6. Fold the pocket/lining piece in half with pocket inside; sew sides starting 3" down from the top edge on each side as shown in Figure 4 to complete the lining; press side seams open as shown in Figure 5.

Figure 4   Figure 5

7. Fold the A panel in half with right sides together; stitch as in step 6. Press side seams open.

8. Turn the A panel right side out; pin the lining inside with wrong side of the lining against the wrong side of the A panel and aligning the 3" side openings as shown in Figure 6; topstitch close to the folded edges at the side openings, catching both the purse top and the lining, again referring to Figure 6.

Figure 6

9. Machine-baste two gathering lines close together along the top edge of one side of the purse catching both the lining and the top of the purse as shown in Figure 7; repeat on the remaining side of the purse. Pull the bobbin threads to gather the top edges to measure 10" on each side as shown in Figure 8.

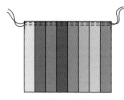

Figure 7   Figure 8

10. Fold each D strip in half with right sides together along length; lay the 2" x 27" batting strip on top. Sew along the 27" raw-edge side. Turn right side out and press flat; topstitch down both long sides to complete the handles.

11. Fold the E strip in half with right sides together along length; stitch along the 5" raw-edge side. Turn right side out and press flat.

12. Place a C strip right side up on the fusible side of a 3½" x 10½" batting strip and fuse in place; fold to crease the center of the strip.

13. Fold the closure loop in half with raw ends together and center on the creased center of the C/batting strip as shown in Figure 9; machine-baste to hold in place.

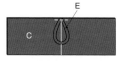

Figure 9

14. Pin and machine-baste a handle strip 1" from each side edge, making sure it is not twisted, as shown in Figure 10.

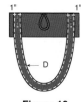

Figure 10   Figure 11

15. Place another C strip right sides together with the C/batting/handle unit and stitch across short ends and along the side with the basted pieces as shown in Figure 11.

16. Turn the unit right side out; press.

17. Pin and stitch one side of the stitched C unit to the top of the right side of the gathered purse using a ½" seam allowance as shown in Figure 12. *Note: Adjust gathering to fit inside the C unit for stitching, if necessary.*

Figure 12   Figure 13

18. Turn the unstitched raw edge of C to the inside ½" and hand-stitch to the lining; topstitch close to the edge around the outer edges of C to finish one top edge as shown in Figure 13.

19. Repeat steps 12 and 14–18 with the second set of C pieces and handle to finish the other top edge.

20. Position and sew the button to the C unit opposite the loop to finish the purse.

Completing the Coin Purse

1. Join the F strips with right sides together along length; press seams in one direction. Trim to 8" x 10".

2. Fuse the 8" x 10" batting rectangle to the wrong side of the F panel and place lining wrong side against batting side.

3. Attach zipper as directed on zipper package along the 8" sides of the rectangles as shown in Figure 14.

Figure 14

4. Fold the G strip in half with right sides together along length; stitch along the 6" raw edge. Turn right side out through an open end; press flat with seam on one side. Topstitch along both edges, if desired.

5. Fold the G strip in half to make a loop; insert and pin between the layers of the quilted tube just below the zipper on the side with the zipper pull.

6. Open the zipper. Fold the tube in half with right sides together and zipper on the top with side edges even as shown in Figure 15; stitch down each side.

Figure 15

7. Turn right side out through zipper opening to finish. ◆

Bag in Blue Purse
Placement Diagram 16" x 12½", excluding handles

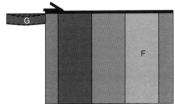

Bag in Blue Coin Purse
Placement Diagram Approximately 9½" x 7½", excluding loop

Fun-to-Cook Apron

Cooking is a lot more fun when you are wearing this bright-color apron stitched from fat quarter strips.

DESIGN BY LORINE MASON

PROJECT SPECIFICATIONS

Skill Level: Beginner
Apron Size: One size fits most

MATERIALS

- 6 fat quarters coordinating bright fabrics
- 1 fat quarter coordinating fabric for pocket lining and binding
- All-purpose thread to match fabrics
- Quilting thread
- 1" button
- 1 package coordinating extra-wide double-fold bias binding
- Basic sewing tools and supplies

Cutting

1. Cut five 2½" x 21" strips from each of the six fat quarters.

2. Cut one 2½" x 8½" strip from each of four fat quarters for pocket.

3. Referring to Figure 1, cut one pocket lining from the coordinating-fabric fat quarter.

Figure 1

4. Cut three 2" x 21" strips from the coordinating-fabric fat quarter for top and side binding.

Completing the Apron

1. Select five strips and cut in half to make (10) 2½" x 10½" strips. **Note:** *You will have more strips than needed to allow for creative placement in a planned or unplanned order.*

2. Select two 10½" strips and join along length; press seam to one side. Topstitch ¼" from seam.

3. Select another 10½" strip, and matching one end even with the edge of a strip, add to the stitched strips as shown in Figure 2; press seam toward the newly added strip.

Figure 2   **Figure 3**

4. Topstitch ¼" from the seam on the newly added strip as shown in Figure 3.

5. Add the remaining 10½" strips to the square corner edges of the pieced section, topstitching ¼" from seam on each strip added as shown in Figure 4.

Figure 4

6. Repeat step 5 with 21"-long strips to add 10 strips to each side.

7. Referring to Figure 5, trim the panel to make the apron shape, positioning the points of the strips at the center of the apron, again referring to Figure 5.

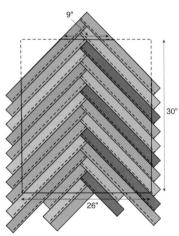

Figure 5

8. Turn the bottom edges under ¼"; press. Turn under again 1" and topstitch for hem.

9. Join the four 2½" x 8½" strips along length; press seams in one direction. Trim unit to 8" x 8". Place wrong sides together with the pocket lining piece; trim corner of pieced unit to match lining.

10. With right sides together, stitch the pieced pocket to the pocket lining all around, leaving a 3" opening on one side; trim corners.

11. Turn pocket right side out; press edges flat. Turn open edges ¼" to the inside, press and hand-stitch opening closed.

12. Turn the top edge of the pocket lining to the front as indicated in Figure 6; press.

Figure 6   Figure 7

13. Stitch a button in the center of the widest part of the folded pocket edge as shown in Figure 7.

14. Pin the pocket to the right-side edge of the apron with bottom of pocket 3" from side edge and top of the pocket 6" from side edge, and the left bottom corner 7" from bottom edge as shown in Figure 8; stitch in place around three sides.

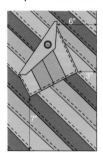

Figure 8

15. Fold each long edge of each fat quarter binding strip to the center wrong side of the strips; fold strips in half and press.

16. Enclose each side and the top edge of the apron inside the binding strips; stitch in place using a machine blanket stitch, catching both sides of the binding in the stitching. Trim ends of binding even with apron. ***Note:*** *Basting these strips in place before stitching assures accurate stitching in this step.*

17. Find the center of bias binding length and mark with pin. Measure 11" on each side of the center and mark. Remove center pin.

18. Open the binding and enclose the angled edge of the apron on each side, positioning the 11" marks at apron top, as shown in Figure 9; stitch in place as in step 16, extending stitching around the neck loop and to the ends of the ties. Make a knot at each end of each tie to finish. ◆

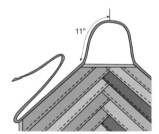

Figure 9

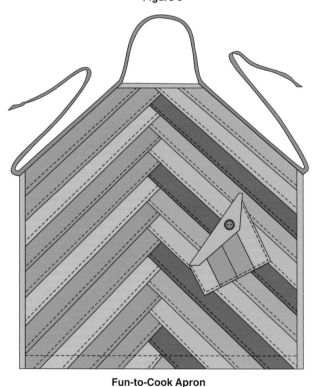

Fun-to-Cook Apron
Placement Diagram One size fits most

Easy Prairie Runner

A border of prairie points add color and zest to this easy table runner.

DESIGN BY NANCY RICHOUX

PROJECT SPECIFICATIONS

Skill Level: Beginner
Runner Size: 36½" x 13½"

MATERIALS

- 2 fat quarters each 4 bright colors
- ⅝ yard each cream mottled and cream tonal
- Batting 45" x 22"
- All-purpose thread to match fabrics
- Quilting thread
- Basic sewing tools and supplies

Cutting

1. Cut one 7¼" by fabric width strip each cream mottled and cream tonal; subcut strips into two 18¾" A pieces each fabric.

2. Cut one 9" by fabric width strip each cream mottled and cream tonal; subcut strips into two 21" backing rectangles each fabric.

3. Cut five 4" x 4" B squares from each of the eight bright-color fat quarters to total 40 B squares.

Completing the Runner

1. Join two different-fabric A pieces along the 18¾" edges as shown in Figure 1; press seam to one side. Repeat to make two A units, pressing seam in the second unit to the opposite side.

Figure 1

2. Join the two A units to complete the pieced center; press seam to one side.

3. Join the four backing rectangles to make a 17½" x 41½" backing piece.

4. Sandwich the batting between the pieced top and pieced backing, matching center seams and fabrics from front to back; pin or baste layers together.

5. Quilt as desired by hand or machine.

6. Trim batting even with quilt top edges; trim backing ¾" wider than the quilt top all around.

7. Fold each B square in half on one diagonal; press. Fold in half again to make a triangle as shown in Figure 2; press. Repeat with all B squares to make a total of 40 B triangles for prairie points.

Figure 2

8. Select color order, and starting at one corner of one long side of the A unit with all B triangles facing the same direction, place 15 B triangles along the edge of the quilted top, repeating color order, and slipping the end of one B into the opening of the previous B as shown in Figure 3 until you reach the opposite end. Reposition as necessary to fit and baste in place.

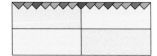

Figure 3

9. Keeping the same color order, place five triangles on the adjacent short end, butting edges as shown in Figure 4; baste in place.

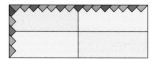

Figure 4

10. Repeat steps 8 and 9 on the remaining side and end of the quilted top.

11. Fold backing edge in ⅜" all around and press. Fold backing to the right side of the runner edges as shown in Figure 5; hand- or machine-stitch in place to finish edges. ◆

Figure 5

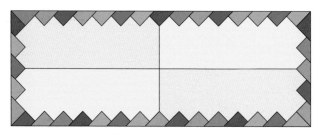

Easy Prairie Runner
Placement Diagram 36½" x 13½"

Christmas Square Tree Skirt

Squares of red and green create an easy Christmas tree skirt.

DESIGN BY NANCY RICHOUX

PROJECT SPECIFICATIONS

Skill Level: Beginner
Tree Skirt Size: 36" x 36"

MATERIALS

- 4 different red tonal fat quarters
- 4 different green tonal fat quarters
- Batting 44" x 44"
- Backing 44" x 44"
- All-purpose thread to match fabrics
- Quilting thread
- 2 packages ¼"-wide red double-fold bias tape
- Water-soluble marker
- Basic sewing tools and supplies

Cutting

1. Assign a number to each red and green fabric (red 1, green 1, red 2, green 2, etc.)—each fabric is referenced by number in the figure drawings.

2. Cut two 5" x 21" strips each red 1, red 2, green 3 and green 4 fabrics; subcut strips into seven 5" squares each fabric.

3. Cut two 5" x 21" strips each red 3, red 4, green 1 and green 2 fabrics; subcut strips into six 5" squares each fabric.

4. Cut one 5⅜" x 21" strip each green 1, green 2, red 3 and red 4; subcut strips into one 5⅜" square each fabric. Cut each square in half on one diagonal to make two triangles each fabric.

Completing the Tree Skirt

Note: Use a ¼" seam allowance and press all seams open.

1. Join one square each red 1, green 1, red 2 and green 2 to make a 1-2 Four-Patch 1-2 unit as shown in Figure 1; press. Repeat to make six 1-2 Four-Patch units.

Figure 1

2. Referring to Figure 2, repeat step 1 with one each red 3, green 3, red 4 and green 4 squares to make six 3-4 Four-Patch units.

Figure 2

3. Sew a red 3 and red 4 triangle to a green 4 square to make a corner unit as shown in Figure 3; press.

Figure 3

4. Repeat step 3 referring to Figure 4 to complete three more corner units.

Figure 4

5. Arrange the Four-Patch and corner units as shown in Figure 5.

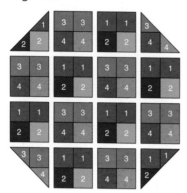

Figure 5

6. Join the units to make four sections as shown in Figure 6; press.

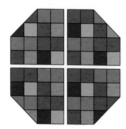

Figure 6

7. Using a straightedge and a rotary cutter, remove the ¼" seam allowance on the inside straight edge of two of the sections as shown in Figure 7.

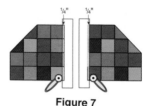

Figure 7

8. Join the sections to complete the pieced top as shown in Figure 8; press.

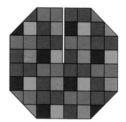

Figure 8

9. Prepare template for the skirt center circle using pattern given.

10. Sandwich batting between the prepared backing and pieced top; pin or baste layers together to hold.

11. Quilt as desired by hand or machine. When quilting is complete, trim excess batting and backing even with edges of the quilted top.

12. Lay the tree-skirt top on a flat surface and center the skirt center circle template on top; mark around circle using a water-soluble marker. Trim circle on marked lines to make skirt center.

13. Bind edges of the tree skirt referring to the instructions given with the packaged bias tape to finish. ◆

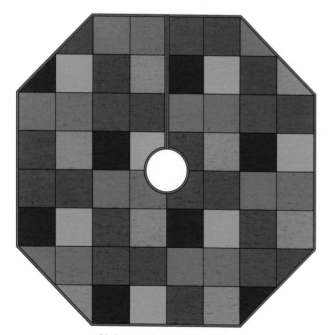

Christmas Square Tree Skirt
Placement Diagram 36" x 36"

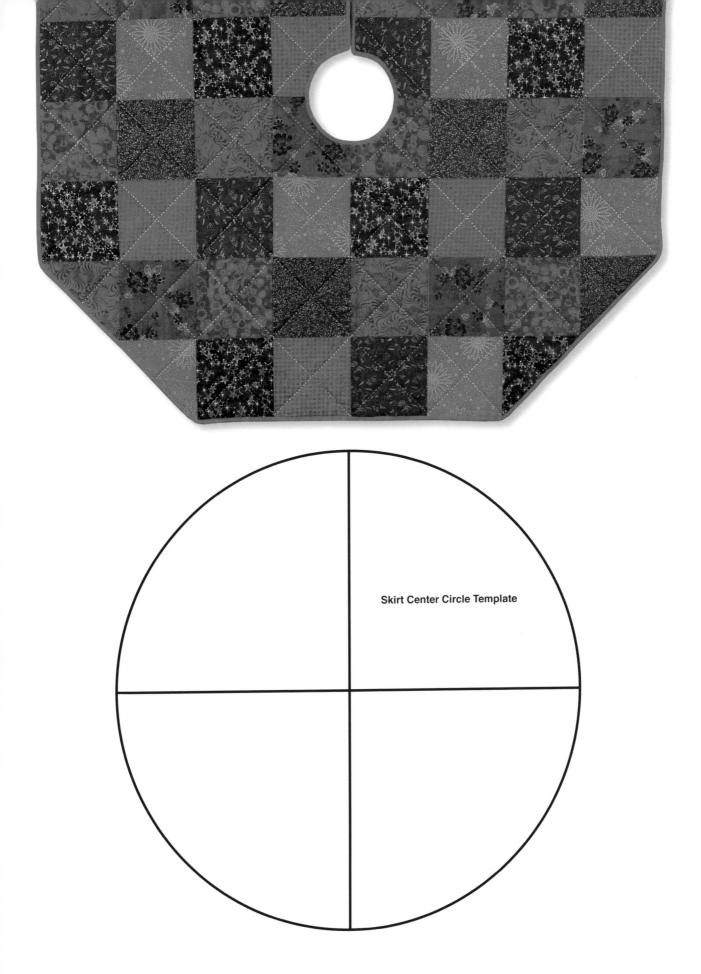

Skirt Center Circle Template

Summer Fixin's

Now you can visit the farmer's market every day!

DESIGN BY CONNIE KAUFFMAN

PROJECT SPECIFICATIONS

Skill Level: Beginner
Quilt Size: 51½" x 63½"

MATERIALS

- 1 fat quarter each tomato, blueberry, orange, potato, beets and grape prints for A
- 1 fat quarter parsley print
- 2 fat quarters lemon print
- ½ yard blackberry print
- ⅔ yard pepper print
- 1⅛ yards basil print
- Batting 60" x 72"
- Backing 60" x 72"
- All-purpose thread to match fabrics
- Quilting thread
- Basic sewing tools and supplies

Cutting

1. Cut (11) 5" x 5" A squares from each of the A fabrics listed.

2. Cut four 5" x 21" strips lemon print; subcut strips into (33) 2" B strips.

3. Cut three 5" x 21" strips parsley print; subcut strips into (22) 2½" C strips.

4. Cut one 5" by fabric width strip pepper print; subcut strip into (11) 2½" D strips.

5. Cut six 2¼" by fabric width strips pepper print for binding.

6. Cut two 2½" by fabric width F strips blackberry print.

7. Cut three 2½" by fabric width E strips blackberry print.

8. Cut six 5½" by fabric width G/H strips basil print.

Completing the Top

1. Arrange and join six A squares with one D, two C and three B strips to make a row as shown in Figure 1; press seams toward A squares. Repeat to make 11 rows.

Figure 1

Continued on page 169

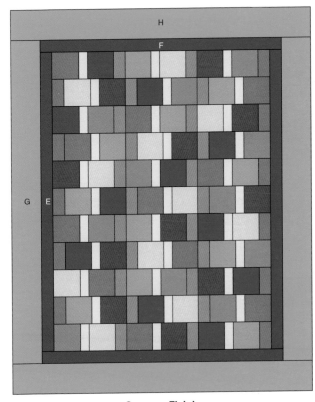

Summer Fixin's
Placement Diagram 51½" x 63½"

Cherry Pickin'

Celebrate spring by quilting this lovely table runner and place mats set. Every meal will become a special occasion.

DESIGNS BY BARBARA MILLER FROM BRENDA/BARB DESIGNS

PROJECT SPECIFICATIONS

Skill Level: Beginner
Runner Size: 58" x 18"
Place Mat Size: 18" x 12"

MATERIALS

- Scraps red mottleds and green mottleds and tonals
- 6 coordinating fat quarters
- 1 fat quarter each light, medium and dark green mottleds
- ⅜ yard white tonal
- ⅞ yard darkest green mottled
- Batting 66" x 26" and (2) 22" x 16"
- Backing 66" x 26" and (2) 22" x 16"
- All-purpose thread to match fabrics and brown
- Quilting thread
- ¼ yard lightweight fusible web
- Basic sewing tools and supplies

Cutting for Runner

1. Cut three 2½" by fabric width strips white tonal; subcut strips into two strips each of the following: 24½" A, 10½" B, 6½" C and 4½" D.

2. Cut (22) total 4½" x 4½" F squares from the coordinating fat quarters.

3. Cut two 4½" x 20½" G strips each light, medium and dark green mottleds.

4. Cut one 6½" by fabric width strip darkest green mottled; subcut into one 6½" E square. Cut two 2¼" strips from the remaining width for binding.

5. Cut three 2¼" by fabric width strips darkest green mottled for additional binding.

Cutting for 2 Place Mats

1. Cut one 2½" by fabric width strip white tonal; subcut strip into two 12½" H strips.

2. Cut two 4½" x 12½" I strips each light, medium and dark green mottleds.

3. Cut six 4½" x 4½" F squares from coordinating fat quarters.

4. Cut four 2¼" by fabric width strips darkest green mottled for binding

Completing the Runner

1. Sew an F square to one end of each G strip; press seams on half toward F and half toward G.

2. Join one each light, medium and dark green F-G strips, alternating seam pressing to make an F-G unit as shown in Figure 1. Repeat to make two F-G units.

Figure 1

3. Join six F squares to make an F strip; press seams in one direction. Repeat to make two F strips.

4. Join one F-G unit and an F strip with an A strip to complete one end unit of the runner as shown

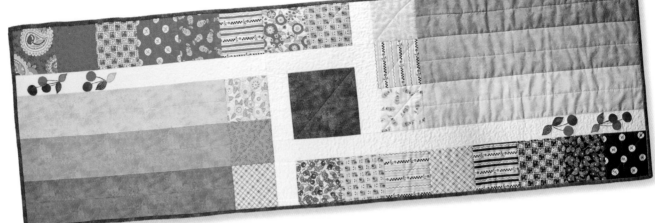

in Figure 2; press seams away from the A strip. Repeat to make a second end unit.

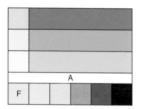

Figure 2

5. Sew C to opposite sides of E; press seams toward E. Sew B to the top and bottom of E to complete the E unit as shown in Figure 3; press seams toward E.

Figure 3

Figure 4

6. Join two F squares with D at one end to make a D-F unit as shown in Figure 4; press seams away from D. Repeat to make two D-F units.

7. Sew a D-F unit to opposite sides of the E unit to complete the center unit as shown in Figure 5; press seams away from the E unit.

Figure 5

8. Sew an end unit to each long side of the center unit to complete the piecing of the runner top.

Appliquéing Cherry Motifs

1. Trace appliqué shapes onto the paper side of the fusible web, leaving ½" between shapes, as directed on pattern; cut out shapes, leaving a margin around each one.

2. Fuse shapes to the wrong side of fabrics as directed on pieces for color; cut out shapes on traced lines. Remove paper backing.

3. Arrange and fuse appliqué motifs on each A strip referring to the Placement Diagram and the appliqué motif pattern for positioning.

4. Using brown thread, machine-stitch several lines of decorative stitching to create the stems between cherries and leaves.

5. Using thread to match fabrics, machine blanket-stitch around each leaf and cherry shape to complete the runner top.

Completing the Place Mats

1. To make one place mat, join three I strips along length to make an I unit; press seams in one direction.

2. Join three F squares to make an F unit; press seams in one direction.

3. Join the I and F units with H referring to the Placement Diagram; press seams away from H to complete the place mat piecing.

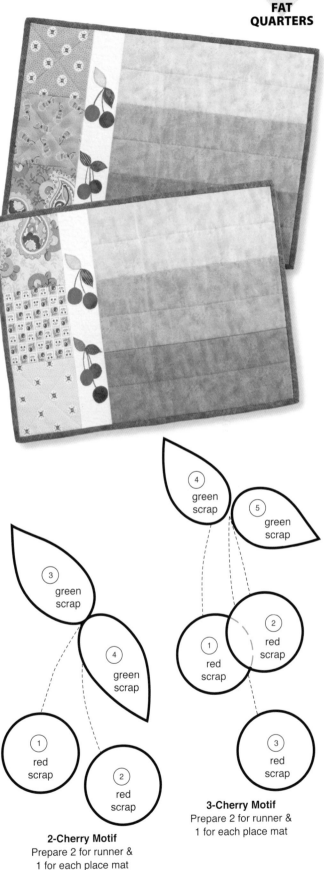

4. Prepare and add appliqué motifs to H referring to Appliquéing Cherry Motifs.

5. Repeat steps 1–4 to complete two place mat tops.

Completing the Runner & Place Mats

1. Sandwich the batting pieces between the completed tops and prepared backing pieces; pin or baste layers together.

2. Quilt as desired by hand or machine. When quilting is complete, trim batting and backing even with edges of the quilted tops.

3. Join binding strips on short ends with diagonal seams to make one long strip; trim seams to ¼" and press seams open. ***Note:*** *You may join the runner strips to make one strip and the place mat strips to make a separate strip, or join them all to make one continuous strip to be used for all projects.*

4. Fold binding strip in half wrong sides together along length; press.

5. Sew binding to the right side of each top, matching raw edges, mitering corners and overlapping ends; press binding away from quilt edges and turn to the back side. Hand- or machine-stitch in place to finish. ◆

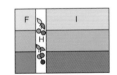

Cherry Pickin' Place Mat
Placement Diagram 18" x 12"

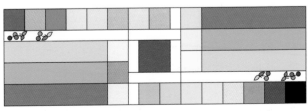

Cherry Pickin' Runner
Placement Diagram 58" x 18"

2-Cherry Motif
Prepare 2 for runner &
1 for each place mat

3-Cherry Motif
Prepare 2 for runner &
1 for each place mat

21-Strip Salute

Try a fun way to select which color comes next by using small paper bags that are coded with letters.

DESIGN BY NANCY VASILCHIK; MACHINE-QULTED BY SUE THARP

PROJECT SPECIFICATIONS

Skill Level: Intermediate
Quilt Size: 85½" x 80"

MATERIALS

- 10 medium–dark fat quarters
- ½ yard medium/dark print for E
- 1⅔ yards black solid
- 3 yards yellow tonal
- Batting 94" x 88"
- Backing 94" x 88"
- All-purpose thread to match fabrics
- Quilting thread
- 11 small brown paper bags
- Basic sewing tools and supplies

Cutting

1. Place each of the 10 fat quarters in a paper bag; close and assign a letter to each bag—A–D and F–K. Place the E fabric into the remaining bag and label E.

2. Select and remove fabric from bag A and cut one 4" x 20½" A1 strip, two 1½" x 20½" A2 strips, and two 4" x 4½" A3 pieces, referring to Figure 1 for cutting layout. Place pieces back in the A bag. *Note: Return all pieces to the appropriate labeled bag after cutting.*

3. Select the B, H and J bags, and referring to Figure 2, cut the following from each fat quarter: two 4" x 16½" for B1, H1 and J1; four 1½" x 20½" for B2, H2 and J2; and four 4" x 6½" for B3, H3 and J3.

4. Select the C, G and K bags, and referring to Figure 3, cut the following from each fat quarter: two 4" x 12½" C1, G1 and K1; four 1½" x 20½ for C2, G2 and K2; and four 4" x 8½" for C3, G3 and K3.

5. Select the D and F bags, and referring to Figure 4, cut the following from each fat quarter: two 4" x 8½" for D1 and F1, four 1½" x 20½" for D2 and F2, and four 4" x 10½" for D3 and F3.

6. Select the I bag, and referring to Figure 5, cut two 4" x 20½" I1 strips, four 1½" x 20½" I2 stips, and four 4" x 4½" I3 pieces.

7. Select the E bag and cut two 1½" by fabric width strips fabric E; subcut four 20½" E2 pieces.

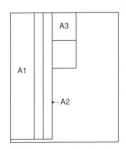

Figure 1

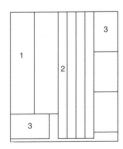

Figure 2

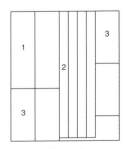

Figure 3

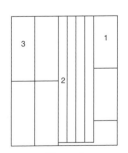

Figure 4

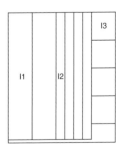

Figure 5

8. Cut two 4" by fabric width strips fabric E; subcut into four 12½" E3 pieces and two 4½" E1 pieces.

9. Cut (42) 1¾" by fabric width strips yellow tonal; subcut each strip into two 20½" X strips.

10. Cut eight 3" by fabric width L/M strips yellow tonal.

11. Cut eight 4" by fabric width N/O strips black solid.

12. Cut nine 2½" by fabric width strips black solid for binding.

Completing the Pieced Strips

1. Sew a 1½" x 20½" A2 strip between two 1¾" x 20½" X strips to make an A2 unit as shown in Figure 6; press seams toward the A2 strip.

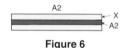

Figure 6

2. Repeat step 1 with all X and lettered No. 2 strips to make two A2 units and four units each B2–K2.

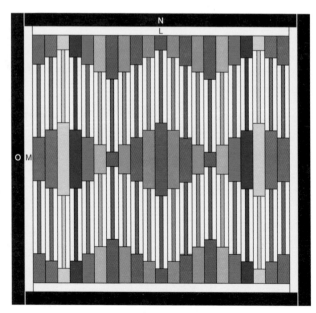

21-Strip Salute
Placement Diagram 85½" x 80"

3. Sew an A2 unit to opposite short ends of A1 and add A3 to each end to make the pieced center strip as shown in Figure 7; press seams away from the A2 units.

Figure 7

4. Repeat step 3 with each lettered B–K No. 1 and No. 3 pieces and the B2–K2 units to complete two each B–K pieced strips referring to Figure 8; press seams away from the No. 2 units in each strip.

Figure 8

Completing the Quilt

1. Arrange and join the pieced strips starting in the center with A, adding a B strip to each side of A as shown in Figure 9; press seams toward B strips.

Figure 9

2. Continue adding strips to each side of the center A-B section in alphabetical order until you have added two strips of each letter, one on each side of A referring to Figure 10; press seams toward the most recently added strips.

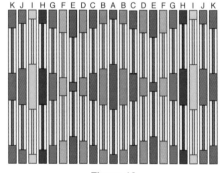

Figure 10

3. Join the L/M strips on short ends to make one long strip; press seams open. Subcut strip into two 74" L strips and two 73½" M strips.

4. Sew the L strips to the top and bottom, and the M strips to the opposite sides of the pieced center; press seams toward L and M strips.

5. Join the N/O strips on short ends to make one long strip; press seams open. Subcut strips into two 79" N strips and two 80½" O strips.

6. Sew the N strips to the top and bottom, and the O strips to the opposite sides of the pieced center to complete the pieced top; press seams toward N and O strips.

No-Wavy Border Tip

To prevent wavy borders, measure the width of the quilt center as shown in Figure 11. Cut and piece two border strips the center measurement. Fold each border strip and the pieced top in half across width and crease to mark the centers. Pin borders to the pieced top, matching creased centers. Pin from the center out to each end, easing if necessary to fit before stitching.

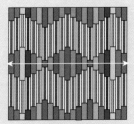

Figure 11

Repeat this process on the remaining sides, measuring through the center perpendicular to the previous center measurement.

Quilt edges may be different lengths because of uneven stretching on each side during stitching, or from inaccurate piecing on the quilt top. If too-long border strips are stitched to the edges and then trimmed, the quilt could end up longer on one side than the other. Measuring through the center of a quilt instead of along each edge prevents border strips from being different sizes and eliminates the wavy look.

Completing the Quilt

1. Sandwich the batting between the completed top and prepared backing; pin or baste layers together.

2. Quilt as desired by hand or machine. When quilting is complete, trim batting and backing even with edges of the quilted top.

3. Join binding strips on short ends with diagonal seams to make one long strip; trim seams to ¼" and press seams open.

4. Fold binding strip in half wrong sides together along length; press.

5. Sew binding to the right side of the top, matching raw edges, mitering corners and overlapping ends; press binding away from quilt edges and turn to the back side. Hand- or machine-stitch in place to finish. ◆

Reversible Flower Pillow

A pillow for a wicker chair or porch swing creates the ideal place to spend a summer evening. Making the pillow reversible will double the pleasure.

DESIGN BY CHRIS MALONE

PROJECT SPECIFICATIONS

Skill Level: Intermediate
Pillow Size: 12" diameter without ruffle and leaves

MATERIALS

- 8 fat quarters medium–dark rose prints
- 1 fat quarter green print
- 1 fat quarter yellow tonal
- Batting 13" x 13" for pillow top and 9" x 16" for leaves
- All-purpose thread to match fabrics
- Quilting thread
- Button or carpet thread
- Long needle
- 2 (1½"-diameter) cover button kits
- Light pink and light green size 8 pearl cotton
- Fiberfill for stuffing
- Basic sewing tools and supplies

Cutting

1. Prepare template for A using pattern given; cut as directed on the piece.

2. Cut one 3" x 12" strip from each of the rose prints for ruffle.

3. Cut one 3" circle each yellow tonal and rose print for cover buttons.

Completing the Pillow

1. Arrange and join the A pieces, joining in sets of two to make quarters, and then join quarters to make halves; join halves to complete the pieced circle as shown in Figure 1. Press seams to one side after stitching each unit. ***Note:*** *You don't need to be overly concerned about making a perfect center because the button will cover this area.*

Figure 1

2. Transfer curved pattern to the center of each A piece using a water-soluble marker.

3. Baste the pieced pillow top on the 13" x 13" batting square; hand-quilt ¼" from each seam joining the A pieces and on the marked lines using light pink size 8 pearl cotton.

4. Trim the batting along the outer edge to match the size of the pieced top.

5. Using the pieced-and-quilted pillow top as a pattern, cut one yellow tonal back piece.

6. To make leaves, trace the leaf pattern given two times on the wrong side of the green print, leaving at least ½" between tracing; fold the fabric in half with right sides together with traced patterns on top.

7. Pin the folded fabric to the 9" x 16" piece of batting and sew all around on the marked lines, leaving open at the bottom edge. Cut out each

leaf ¼" from the seam; trim batting close to seam. Trim tips and clip curves; turn right side out and press edges flat.

8. Transfer leaf quilting lines referring to the leaf pattern.

9. Hand-quilt ¼" from edge and on marked lines on each leaf using light green size 8 pearl cotton.

10. Join the ruffle strips with diagonal seams to make one long strip as shown in Figure 2; trim seams to ¼" and press open.

Figure 2

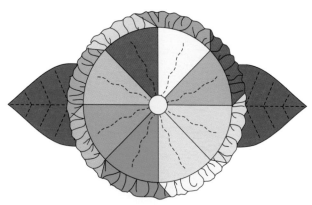

Reversible Flower Pillow
Placement Diagram 12" diameter without ruffle and leaves

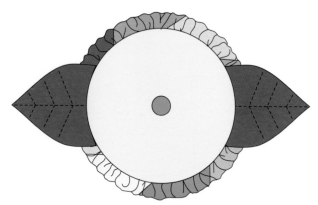

Reversible Flower Pillow
Placement Diagram 12" diameter without ruffle and leaves

11. Join the strips to form one large circle as shown in Figure 3; press the ruffle circle strip in half along length with wrong sides together to make a double-layered ruffle.

Figure 3

12. Sew a line of machine gathering stitches ¼" from the raw edges of the folded ruffle strip. **Note:** *Do not backstitch at the beginning or end.* Sew a second gathering line ⅛" from the raw edges.

13. Divide the ruffle into quarters; mark with pins. Pull on the two bobbin threads of the gathering lines to gather the ruffle. Match and pin each quarter mark to a quarter of the pillow top (two A wedges) as shown in Figure 4. When the ruffle fits the circle, tie off the gathering thread ends and adjust the gathers where needed to evenly distribute the ruffle; machine-baste in place to hold and remove pins.

Figure 4

14. Pin a leaf to one side of the pillow top on top of the ruffle, aligning the leaf center with a seam between two A pieces and matching raw edges as shown in Figure 5; carefully baste the curved seams. Repeat with second leaf on the opposite side.

Figure 5

15. Pin the yellow tonal backing circle right sides together over the pinned pillow top unit; sew all around, leaving a 5" opening. Turn the pillow right side out through the opening, extending the leaves outward.

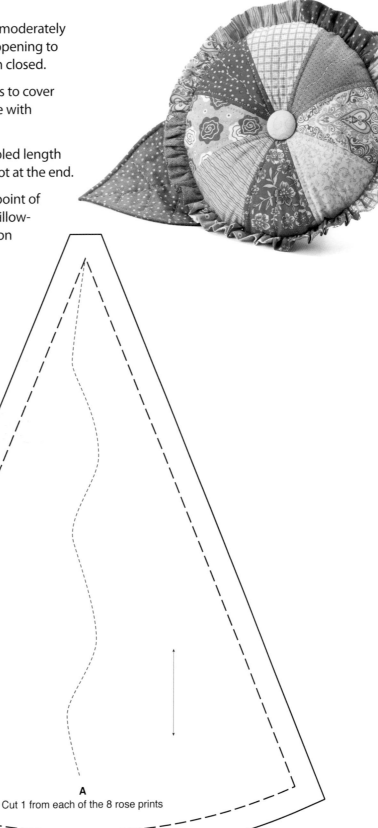

16. Stuff the pillow with fiberfill until moderately firm; fold the seam allowance of the opening to the inside ¼" and securely hand-stitch closed.

17. Follow manufacturer's instructions to cover one button with yellow tonal and one with rose print.

18. Thread a long needle with a doubled length of button or carpet thread; make a knot at the end.

19. Insert the needle into the center point of the pillow back and come up at the pillow-top center. Add the yellow tonal button to the threaded needle and go back into the pillow, coming out at the center back.

20. Pick up the rose print button and return to the top; pull slightly to indent pillow on both sides. Make another stitch through the shank of the yellow button and return to the back. Pull gently again; knot and clip thread to finish. ◆

A
Cut 1 from each of the 8 rose prints

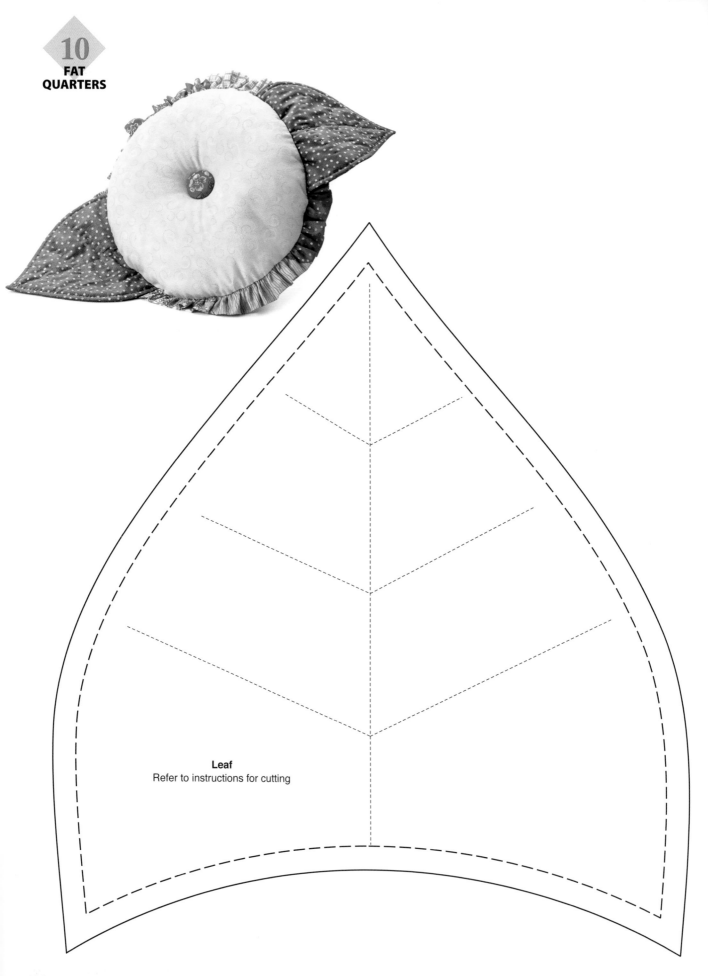

Leaf
Refer to instructions for cutting

Zoo-Friendly Packs

Smiley lion and a blushing giraffe will soon be best friends with the children who receive these small bags, perfect for toys and books.

DESIGN BY LORINE MASON

PROJECT SPECIFICATIONS

Skill Level: Intermediate
Pack Size: Approximately 15¼" x 9"

MATERIALS

Note: *Materials given make one pack.*
- 11 coordinating fat quarters
- (2) 12" x 18" rectangles and (1) 7½" x 7½" square lightweight cotton batting
- Neutral-color all-purpose thread
- Black embroidery floss
- 1 yard ½" nylon strapping
- Black and white felt scraps
- ¼ yard lightweight fusible web
- Permanent black fabric marker
- 2 (⅝") wooden beads
- Appliqué pressing sheet
- Large safety pin
- Basic sewing tools and supplies

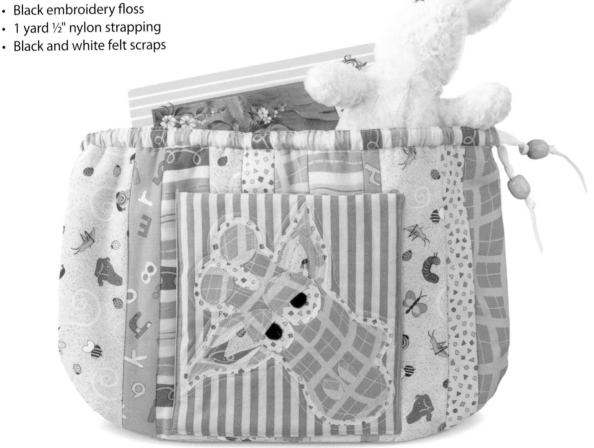

Cutting

1. Prepare a template for the pack using the pattern given on page 170, enlarging 200%; cut one lining piece from each of two fabrics.

2. Cut one 7½" x 15" rectangle any fat quarter for pocket.

3. Set aside one fat quarter for backing. Cut strips from the remaining fat quarters alternating widths from 1" to 1½" to 2" wide.

Completing the Pack

1. Using the prepared template, loosely trim the two 12" x 18" rectangles of cotton batting approximately 1" larger than the pattern all around.

2. Lay one cotton-batting piece on a flat surface and draw a straight vertical line down the left side 1" from the left edge as shown in Figure 1.

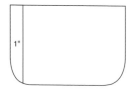

Figure 1

3. Lay a 1"-wide strip right side up along the marked line. Place a second strip right side down on top of the first strip and pin through all layers.

4. Stitch using a ¼" seam as shown in Figure 2; press the strip to the right side.

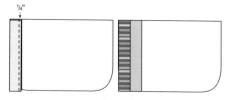

Figure 2

5. Continue adding strips in this manner, alternating width of strips for variety, until the batting surface is covered. Pin the bag template on top of the stitched layers and trim even with template; set aside.

6. Place the fat quarter set aside for backing right side up on top of the second piece of batting cut in step 1; trim the backing piece even with batting edges.

7. Mark a vertical line 1" from the left edge; topstitch through the fabric and batting, stitching along the marked line. Continue stitching in this manner, alternating widths between stitching for variety, across the whole back to secure layers together.

8. Trim the backing layers to size using the prepared template.

Completing Appliquéd Pocket

1. Trace appliqué shapes from the lion or giraffe motif on the paper side of the lightweight fusible web, leaving ½" between pieces. Cut out shapes, leaving a margin around each one.

2. Select fabrics from the fat quarters to be used for appliqué pieces, referring to the project samples for color-placement suggestions. Fuse shapes to the wrong side of the chosen fabrics.

3. Cut out shapes on traced lines; remove paper backing.

4. Cut eye pieces from black and/or white felt.

5. Place the appliqué motif under the appliqué pressing sheet.

6. Arrange and fuse fabric pieces to complete the chosen motif in numerical order referring to the pattern for placement. When cool, remove motif from pressing sheet.

7. Fold the 7½" x 15" pocket rectangle in half with wrong sides together to make a 7½" x 7½" double layer. Lay it on an ironing board with the folded edge along the top.

8. Arrange and fuse the appliqué motif in the center of the folded pocket.

9. Unfold the fused pocket and refold with right sides together; lay the 7½" cotton batting square on top and stitch around the outside edges, leaving a 3" opening along one side.

10. Trim corners and turn right side out through the opening; press edges flat. Press opening edges to the inside and hand-stitch in place.

11. Topstitch each appliqué piece in place close to the edges using neutral-color all-purpose thread.

12. Center the stitched pocket ¾" from bottom edge on the pack front referring to Figure 3 and stitch in place.

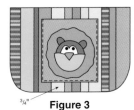

¾" **Figure 3**

Completing the Pack

1. With right sides together, stitch the quilted back to the front, leaving the top edge open; turn right side out and press flat.

2. With right sides together, stitch the two lining pieces together, leaving top edge open and a 3" opening along the bottom edge.

3. Insert the stitched pack into the lining with right sides together; stitch around the top edge as shown in Figure 4.

3" **Figure 4**

4. Turn right side out through the opening in the bottom of the lining; close the opening in the lining by hand or machine.

5. Tuck the lining inside of the bag, letting it extend ½" above the top quilted edge as shown in Figure 5; press and pin to hold.

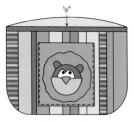

Figure 5

Figure 6

6. Topstitch close to the top folded edge and then again next to the seam line between the lining and the outer shell as shown in Figure 6.

7. Using a seam ripper, carefully open the side seam of the extended lining between the two lines of topstitching to create a casing for the straps as shown in Figure 7.

Figure 7

8. Cut 1 yard of strapping; attach a large safety pin to the end of one piece and insert in the opening created in step 7. Feed the strapping through the casing completely around the bag, exiting through the opening referring to Figure 8.

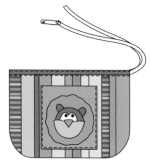

Figure 8

9. Tie a knot in each end of each strap approximately 1" from where the straps exit the bag casing as shown in Figure 9.

Figure 9

10. Slide a bead close to the knot onto each knotted end; knot below each bead again to hold beads in place. Trim excess ends 1" from knots.

11. For lion pack only, use black embroidery floss to stitch whiskers on each side of the lion's muzzle and a fabric pen to add the mouth and ear accents. ◆

Template on page 170

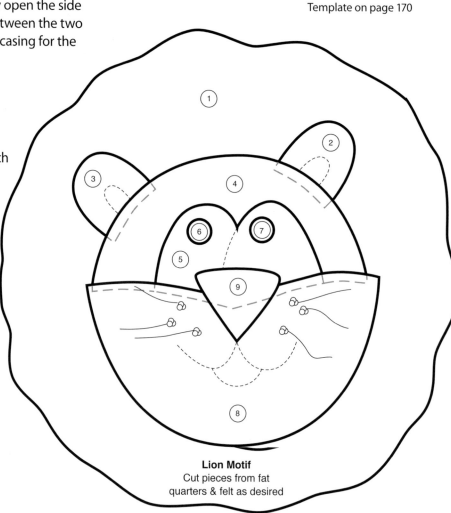

Lion Motif
Cut pieces from fat
quarters & felt as desired

Zoo-Friendly Lion Pack
Placement Diagram Approximately 15¼" x 9"

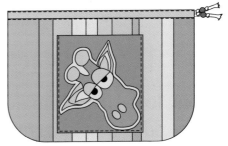

Zoo-Friendly Giraffe Pack
Placement Diagram Approximately 15¼" x 9"

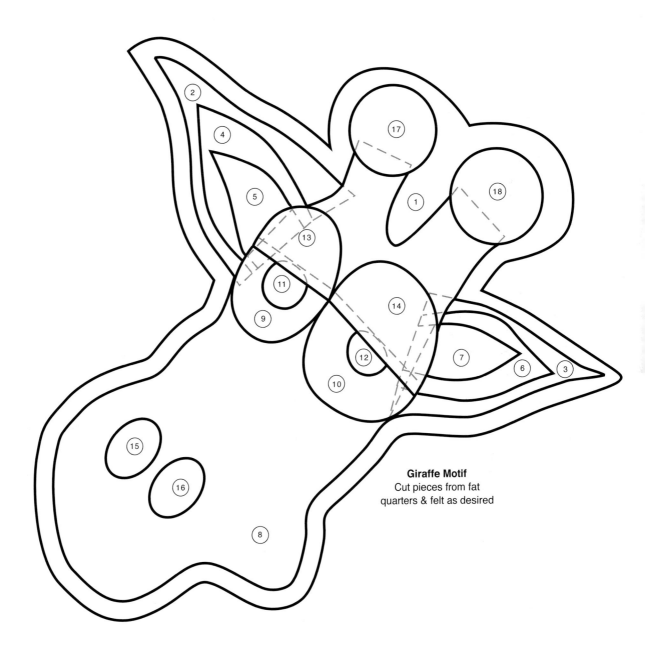

Giraffe Motif
Cut pieces from fat
quarters & felt as desired

Winter Friends

Everyone loves a snowman, and when they smile at you, the whole world is a wonderful place to be.

DESIGN BY JULIE WEAVER

....

PROJECT SPECIFICATIONS

Skill Level: Intermediate
Quilt Size: 22" x 35"
Block Size: 6" x 8"
Number of Blocks: 6

MATERIALS

- Scraps orange and black tonals
- 1 fat quarter cream tonal
- 1 fat quarter tan print
- 1 fat quarter green plaid
- 1 fat quarter red plaid
- 1 fat quarter gold print
- 2 fat quarters blue prints
- 2 fat quarters green prints
- 2 fat quarters red prints
- ½ yard navy print
- Batting 30" x 43"
- Backing 30" x 43"
- Neutral-color and black all-purpose thread
- Quilting thread
- Black embroidery floss
- ⅛ yard lightweight fusible web
- Water-soluble marker
- Basic sewing tools and supplies

Cutting

1. Cut two 4" x 21" strips cream tonal; subcut strips into six 6½" A rectangles.

2. Cut five 1½" x 21" strips tan print; subcut strips into (36) 1½" B squares and (12) 2½" F rectangles.

3. Cut one 2" x 21" strip each red and green plaids; subcut strips into three 6½" C strips each fabric.

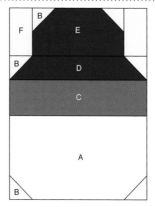

Snowman
6" x 8" Block
Make 6

4. From each blue, green and red print fat quarter, cut one 1½" x 6½" D strip and one 2½" x 4½" E rectangles.

5. Cut eight 1½" x 21" strips gold print; subcut strips into nine 8½" G strips and eight 6½" H strips.

6. Cut one 1½" x 21" strip from one red print; subcut strip into (12) 1½" I squares.

7. Cut one 3½" x 21" strip from the same red print; subcut strip into four 3½" O squares and four 1" x 1" J squares.

8. Using the remaining fat quarters, cut a total of (24) 1½" x 3½" N rectangles and (44) 2" x 3½" M rectangles.

9. Cut two 1" x 28½" K strips navy print.

10. Cut one 1" by fabric width strip navy print; subcut strip into two 15½" L strips.

11. Cut three 2¼" by fabric width strips navy print for binding.

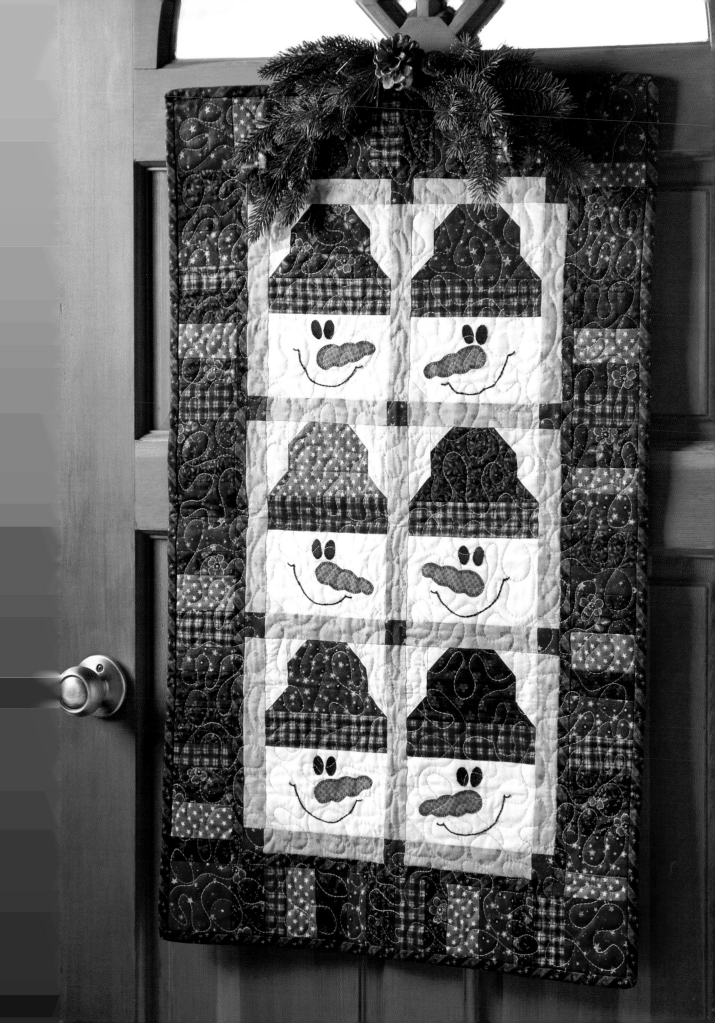

Completing the Blocks

1. Mark a diagonal line from corner to corner on the wrong side of each B square.

2. Place a B square on two corners of A and stitch on the marked line as shown in Figure 1.

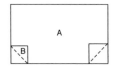

Figure 1

3. Trim seam allowance on each corner to ¼" and press B to the right side to complete an A-B unit as shown in Figure 2. Repeat to make six A-B units.

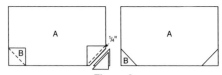

Figure 2

4. Repeat steps 2 and 3 with B on each end of D and on two corners of E as shown in Figure 3 to make six each B-D and B-E units.

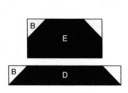

Figure 3   **Figure 4**

5. To complete one Snowman block, sew a C strip between an A-B unit and a B-D unit to make the bottom unit as shown in Figure 4; press seams toward C.

6. Sew an F rectangle to each short end of a B-E unit to complete the hat unit as shown in Figure 5; press seams toward F.

Figure 5

7. Sew the hat unit to the bottom unit referring to the block drawing to complete one pieced block; press seams toward the bottom unit.

8. Repeat steps 5–7 to complete six pieced blocks.

9. Trace nose and eye appliqué shapes onto the paper side of the lightweight fusible web as directed on pieces for cutting, leaving at least ⅛" between pieces. Cut out shapes, leaving a margin around each one.

10. Fuse shapes to fabric scraps as directed on each piece for color; cut out shapes on traced lines. Remove paper backing.

11. Arrange and fuse the nose and eye shapes on A referring to the Placement Diagram and full-size pattern given for positioning. ***Note:*** *Three blocks have noses and mouths facing right and three facing left.*

12. Using black thread and a machine blanket stitch, sew around each fused shape on each block.

13. Place each stitched block on the snowman face pattern, and using a water-soluble marker, transfer mouth shape to each fused block.

14. Using 3 strands black embroidery floss and an outline or stem stitch, stitch along marked line to make mouth shapes to complete the blocks.

Completing the Top

1. Join three same-facing Snowman blocks with four H strips to make a vertical row as shown in Figure 6; press seams toward H. Repeat to make two vertical rows.

2. Join three G strips with four I squares to make a sashing row; press seams toward G strips. Repeat to make three sashing rows.

3. Join the block rows with the sashing rows to complete the pieced center referring to the Placement Diagram for positioning of rows; press seams toward sashing rows.

Figure 6

4. Sew K strips to opposite long sides of the pieced center; press seams toward K strips.

5. Sew a J square to each end of each L strip; press seams toward L.

6. Sew a J-L strip to the top and bottom of the pieced center; press seams toward J-L strips.

7. Sew an N piece between two M pieces to make an N-M unit; press seams away from N. Repeat to make 20 N-M units.

8. Join six N-M units and add one N and one M piece to each end to make a side strip as shown in Figure 7; press seams in one direction. Repeat to make two side strips.

Figure 7

9. Sew a side strip to opposite sides of the pieced center referring to the Placement Diagram for positioning of strips; press seam allowances toward K strips.

10. Join four N-M units and add an O square to each end to make the top strip as shown in Figure 8; press seams toward O. Repeat to make the bottom strip.

Figure 8

11. Sew the top and bottom strips to the top and bottom of the pieced center to complete the pieced top; press seams toward the pieced strips.

Completing the Quilt

1. Sandwich the batting piece between the completed top and prepared backing; pin or baste layers together.

2. Quilt as desired by hand or machine. When quilting is complete, trim batting and backing even with edges of the quilted top.

3. Join binding strips on short ends with diagonal seams to make one long strip; trim seams to ¼" and press seams open.

4. Fold binding strip in half wrong sides together along length; press.

5. Sew binding to the right side of the pieced top, matching raw edges, mitering corners and overlapping ends; press binding away from quilt edges and turn to the back side. Hand- or machine-stitch in place to finish. ◆

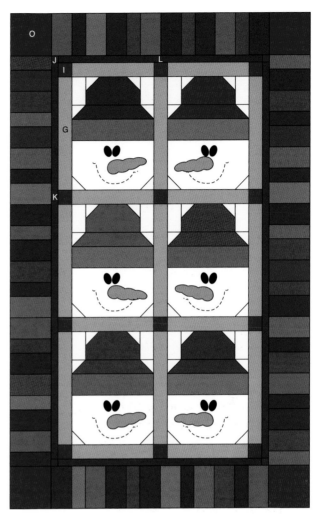

Winter Friends
Placement Diagram 22" x 35"

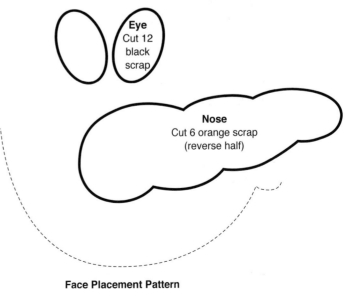

Eye
Cut 12
black
scrap

Nose
Cut 6 orange scrap
(reverse half)

Face Placement Pattern
Reverse 3 faces

Sewing Room Boutique

Stitch this quilt to brighten a corner in your sewing room, or use the alternate flower motif to add a cheery touch to any room.

DESIGN BY CHRIS MALONE

PROJECT NOTES

An alternate flower motif is given that may be appliquéd on the corner squares instead of the pincushion motif. Refer to the photo of the sample for color suggestions.

PROJECT SPECIFICATIONS

Skill Level: Intermediate
Quilt Size: 32" x 32"
Block Size: 6" x 6"
Number of Blocks: 13

MATERIALS

- 1 fat quarter each red, dark green, light green, orange, pink, purple, blue, turquoise and yellow tonals
- 1 fat quarter medium brown mottled
- 1 fat quarter each light brown and dark brown prints
- ¾ yard light tan dot
- Batting 40" x 40"
- Backing 40" x 40"
- All-purpose thread to match fabrics and rickrack
- Black thread
- Quilting thread
- 12 (⁷⁄₁₆") cover button kits
- 12 (¼") black buttons
- 1 package (2½ yards) medium green rickrack
- ¼ yard lightweight fusible web
- Fabric glue stick
- Basic sewing tools and supplies

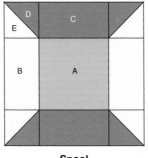

Spool
6" x 6" Block
Make 9

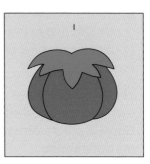

Pincushion
6" x 6" Block
Make 4

Cutting

1. Cut one 3½" x 3½" A square from each of the nine tonal fat quarters.

2. Cut two 5½"-diameter yo-yo circles from each of the following tonal fat quarters: red, orange, pink, purple, blue and turquoise.

3. Cut one 3½" by fabric width strip light tan dot; subcut strip into (18) 2" B rectangles.

4. Cut two 2⅜" by fabric width strips light tan dot; subcut strips into (18) 2⅜" squares. Cut each square in half on one diagonal to make 36 E triangles.

5. Cut two 6½" by fabric width strips light tan dot; subcut strips into four 20½" H strips.

6. Cut three 2⅜" x 21" strips medium brown mottled; subcut strips into (18) 2⅜" squares. Cut each square in half on one diagonal to make 36 D triangles.

7. Cut two 3½" x 21" strips medium brown mottled; subcut strips into (18) 2" C rectangles.

8. Cut two 6½" x 21" strips light brown print; subcut strips into four 6½" I squares.

9. Cut two 1½" x 18½" F strips and two 1½" x 20½" G strips dark brown print.

10. Cut enough 2¼"-wide strips of varying lengths from the light and dark green tonals to make 138" of binding.

Completing the Spool Blocks

1. Sew a D triangle to an E triangle to make a D-E unit as shown in Figure 1; press seam toward D. Repeat to make 36 D-E units.

Figure 1

2. To complete one Spool block, sew a D-E unit to opposite ends of C to make a C row as shown in Figure 2; press seams toward C. Repeat to make two C rows.

Make 2

Figure 2

3. Sew B to two opposite sides of A to make the center row as shown in Figure 3; press seams toward B.

Figure 3

4. Sew a C row to opposite sides of the center row to complete one Spool block referring to the block drawing; press seams toward the center row.

5. Repeat steps 2–4 to complete nine Spool blocks.

Completing the Pincushion Blocks

1. Trace the pincushion shapes on page 171 onto the paper side of the fusible web four times, leaving a ½" space between shapes; cut out shapes, leaving a margin around each one.

2. Fuse shapes to the wrong side of fabrics as directed on pieces for color; cut out shapes on traced lines. Remove paper backing.

3. Fold and crease each I square to mark the horizontal and vertical centers.

4. Center and fuse a pincushion motif on each I square layering pieces in numerical order as marked on patterns.

5. Machine blanket-stitch around each shape using thread to match fabrics to complete the Pincushion blocks.

Completing the Top

1. Arrange and join the Spool blocks in three rows of three blocks each; rotate every other block 90 degrees so some spools appear to be on their sides. Press seams in adjacent rows in opposite directions.

2. Join the rows to complete the pieced center; press seams in one direction.

3. Sew an F strip to opposite sides and G strips to the top and bottom of the pieced center; press seams toward F and G strips.

4. Cut the rickrack into four equal lengths. Arrange a piece in a gentle curve along the center of each H strip referring to the Placement Diagram; tack in place using a fabric glue stick. Stitch each piece of rickrack in place down the center using matching thread. Trim excess at each end of each strip.

5. Sew an H strip to opposite sides of the pieced center; press seams toward H strips.

6. Sew a Pincushion block to each end of each remaining H strip, keeping the blocks upright in the same direction referring to the Placement Diagram; press seams toward blocks.

7. Sew a block/H strip to the top and bottom of the pieced center, keeping Pincushion blocks upright; press seams toward the block/H strips to complete the top.

Completing the Quilt

1. Sandwich the batting between the completed top and prepared backing; pin or baste layers together.

2. Quilt as desired by hand or machine. When quilting is complete, trim batting and backing even with edges of the quilted top. ***Note:*** *The sample quilt has four uneven lines stitched through the center of each Spool block, in the ditch of all seams, around pincushion shapes and ½" from each side of the rickrack.*

3. Using black thread, stitch three sets of long lines on each pincushion to simulate pins referring to the pattern for positioning suggestions.

4. Join the binding strips on short ends with diagonal seams to make one long two-toned strip; trim seams to ¼" and press seams open.

5. Fold binding strip in half wrong sides together along length; press.

6. Sew binding to the right side of the pieced top, matching raw edges, mitering corners and overlapping ends; press binding away from quilt edges and turn to the back side. Hand- or machine-stitch in place.

7. To make a yo-yo, turn under ⅛" all around the edges of a yo-yo circle; begin gathering stitches close to the fold using a doubled length of matching thread as shown in Figure 4. Sew all around the circle, finger-pressing the turned edges as you sew. Pull the stitches tightly to gather and close the circle, again referring to

Figure 4; smooth and flatten the circle with the hole in the center. Knot and clip the thread to complete one yo-yo, again referring to Figure 4. Repeat to make 12 yo-yos in the six colors.

8. Follow manufacturer's instructions to cover the 12 button kits with yellow tonal.

9. Arrange and pin three yo-yos on each H border strip—two on the inside edge of the rickrack and one on the outside edge of the rickrack referring to the Placement Diagram for positioning.

10. Sew a yellow covered button in the center of each yo-yo, attaching the yo-yo to the quilt at the same time. Remove pins.

11. Sew a black button to the top of each simulated pin on the pincushion appliqué to finish. ◆

Patterns on page 171

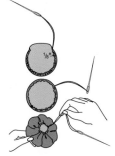

Figure 4

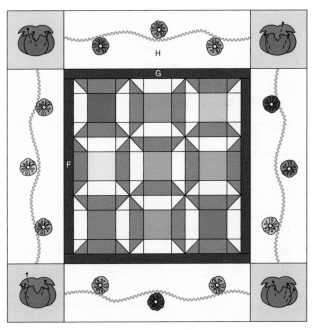

Sewing Room Boutique
Placement Diagram 32" x 32"

Floating Gems

This fun quilt is great for a kid's room. Select fat quarters in brights to represent the floating gems and use neutrals or tonals as the background to make them shine.

DESIGN BY JUDITH SANDSTROM

PROJECT SPECIFICATIONS

Skill Level: Intermediate
Quilt Size: 66" x 90
Block Size: 12" x 12"
Number of Blocks: 35

MATERIALS

- 5 fat quarters assorted tonals
- 7 fat quarters bright-color prints
- ⅔ yard purple mottled
- 1 yard black floral
- 2 yards black tonal
- 2⅓ yards white tonal
- Batting 74" x 98"
- Backing 74" x 98"
- All-purpose thread to match fabrics
- Quilting thread
- Basic sewing tools and supplies

Cutting

1. Cut two 7¼" x 21" strips from each of the tonal fat quarters; subcut strips into (18) 7¼" squares total. Cut each square on both diagonals to make 18 sets of four F triangles. Trim the remainder of each strip into two 3½"-wide strips; set aside.

2. Cut three 3½" x 21" strips from each of the bright-color print fat quarters; subcut these strips and the 3½" trimmed strips from step 1 into a total of (140) 3½" D squares.

3. Cut three 6½" by fabric width strips black tonal; subcut strips into (17) 6½" A squares.

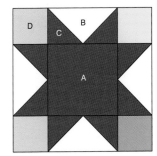

Eight-Pointed Star
12" x 12" Block
Make 17

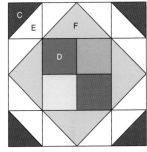

Framed Four-Patch
12" x 12" Block
Make 18

4. Cut (11) 3⅞" by fabric width strips black tonal; subcut strips into (104) 3⅞" squares. Cut each square in half on one diagonal to make 208 C triangles.

5. Cut five 7¼" by fabric width strips white tonal; subcut strips into (23) 7¼" squares. Cut each square on both diagonals to make 92 B triangles.

6. Cut (11) 3⅞" by fabric width strips white tonal; subcut strips into (108) 3⅞" squares. Cut each square in half on one diagonal to make 216 E triangles.

7. Cut three 3⅞" by fabric width strips black floral; subcut strips into (24) 3⅞" squares. Cut each square in half on one diagonal to make 48 G triangles.

8. Cut one 3½" by fabric width strip black floral; subcut strip into four 3½" H squares.

9. Cut two 6½" by fabric width strips black floral; subcut strips into (24) 3½" I rectangles.

10. Cut eight 2½" by fabric width strips purple mottled for binding.

Completing the Eight-Pointed Star Blocks

Note: *All seams are ¼" and are pressed open after stitching.*

1. Sew C to the short sides of B to complete a B-C unit as shown in Figure 1; repeat to make 68 B-C units.

Figure 1   Figure 2

2. To complete one Eight-Pointed Star block, sew a B-C unit to opposite sides of A as shown in Figure 2.

3. Sew D to opposite ends of a B-C unit to make the top row as shown in Figure 3; repeat to make the bottom row.

Figure 3

Floating Gems
Placement Diagram 66" x 90"

4. Sew the top and bottom rows to the center row referring to the block drawing to complete one Eight-Pointed Star block.

5. Repeat steps 2–4 to complete 17 Eight-Pointed Star blocks.

Completing the Framed Four-Patch Blocks

Note: *All seams are ¼" and are pressed open after stitching.*

1. Select four D squares; join two to make a row; repeat to make two rows. Join the rows as shown in Figure 4 to make a D unit; repeat to make 18 D units.

Figure 4

2. Sew E to each short side of F as shown in Figure 5 to make an E-F unit; repeat to make 72 E-F units.

Figure 5   Figure 6

3. Sew C to E along the diagonal to make a C-E unit as shown in Figure 6; repeat to make 72 C-E units.

4. To complete one Framed Four-Patch block, sew an E-F unit to opposite sides of a D unit to make the center row as shown in Figure 7.

Figure 7

5. Sew a C-E unit to opposite ends of an E-F unit to make the top row as shown in Figure 8; repeat to make the bottom row.

Figure 8

6. Sew the top and bottom rows to the center row to complete one Framed Four-Patch block referring to the block drawing.

7. Repeat steps 4–6 to complete 18 Framed Four-Patch blocks.

Completing the Top

Note: *All seams are ¼" and are pressed open after stitching.*

1. Arrange and join two Eight-Pointed Star blocks with three Framed Nine-Patch blocks to make an X row as shown in Figure 9; repeat to make four X rows.

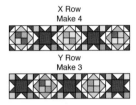

X Row
Make 4

Y Row
Make 3

Figure 9

2. Arrange and join two Framed Nine-Patch blocks with three Eight-Pointed Star blocks to make a Y row, again referring to Figure 9; repeat to make three Y rows.

3. Join the X and Y rows, beginning and ending with an X row to complete the pieced center.

4. Sew G to each short side of B to make a B-G unit as shown in Figure 10; repeat to make 24 B-G units.

Figure 10

5. Join two H squares with four I rectangles and five B-G units to make the top border strip as shown in Figure 11; repeat to make the bottom border strip.

H
Make 2

Make 2
I

Figure 11

6. Sew the top and bottom border strips to the pieced center referring to the Placement Diagram for positioning of strips.

7. Join seven B-G units and eight I rectangles to make a side border strip; repeat to make two strips, as shown in Figure 11.

8. Sew a side border strip to opposite long sides of the pieced center to complete the pieced top.

Completing the Quilt

1. Sandwich the batting between the completed top and prepared backing; pin or baste layers together.

2. Quilt as desired by hand or machine. When quilting is complete, trim batting and backing even with edges of the quilted top.

3. Join binding strips on short ends with diagonal seams to make one long strip; trim seams to ¼" and press seams open.

4. Fold binding strip in half wrong sides together along length; press.

5. Sew binding to the right side of the top, matching raw edges, mitering corners and overlapping ends; press binding away from quilt edges and turn to the back side. Hand- or machine-stitch in place to finish. ◆

Oriental Lanterns

If you love oriental prints, this throw is a good way to use them.

DESIGN BY BEA YURKERWICH

PROJECT SPECIFICATIONS

Skill Level: Beginner
Quilt Size: 40" x 52"
Block Size: 8" x 10"
Number of Blocks: 12

MATERIALS

- 12 fat quarters Oriental prints
- ⅔ yard black solid
- ¾ yard Oriental print
- 1⅛ yards red tonal
- Batting 48" x 60"
- Backing 48" x 60"
- Neutral-color all-purpose thread
- Quilting thread
- Gold metallic thread
- Basic sewing tools and supplies

Cutting

1. Cut one 8½" x 6½" A rectangle each fat quarter.

2. Cut six 2½" by fabric width strips red tonal; subcut strips into (96) 2½" B squares.

3. Cut three 1½" by fabric width C strips red tonal.

4. Cut four 2½" x 40½" E strips red tonal.

5. Cut two 2½" x 32½" F strips red tonal.

6. Cut three 1½" by fabric width D strips black solid.

7. Cut six 2¼" by fabric width strips black solid for binding.

8. Cut three 4½" by fabric width strips Oriental print for G.

9. Cut two 4½" x 40½" H strips Oriental print.

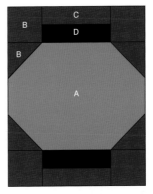

Oriental Lantern
8" x 10" Block
Make 12

Completing the Blocks

1. Mark a diagonal line from corner to corner on the wrong side of 48 B squares.

2. Place a marked B square on each corner of A and stitch on the marked line as shown in Figure 1.

Figure 1

3. Trim seam allowance on each corner to ¼" and press B to the right side to complete an A-B unit as shown in Figure 2. Repeat to make 12 A-B units.

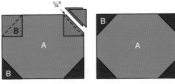

Figure 2

Continued on page 172

Personality Prayer Shawl

Fabric swaps with friends, whether in person or on the Internet, are great places to start collecting fabrics for this shawl. As you collect fabric, you are also collecting prayers.

DESIGN BY JULIA DUNN

PROJECT SPECIFICATIONS

Skill Level: Intermediate
Shawl Size: 70" x 21"
Block Size: 7" x 7"
Number of Blocks: 22

MATERIALS

- 6 fat quarters each black-on-white and white-on-black prints
- ½ yard black-on-white floral
- 1⅝ yards white-on-black floral
- Batting 78" x 29" and two 29" x 22"
- Backing 78" x 29" and two 29" x 22"
- All-purpose thread to match fabrics
- Quilting thread
- 6" white nylon zipper
- Basic sewing tools and supplies

Cutting

1. To cut pieces for one block, from fat quarters select one black-on-white print (light) and one white-on-black print (dark). Cut two of A and B squares and one of each of the remaining squares from each fabric: 1¾" x 1¾" for A (light) and B (dark). Cut one of the following size squares from each fabric: 2⅝" x 2⅝" for C (light) and D (dark); 3⅜" x 3⅜" for E (light) and F (dark); and 4⅜" x 4⅜" for G (light) and H (dark). Cut squares C–H in half on one diagonal to make two triangles each letter. Repeat instructions for 22 block sets.

2. Cut four 1½" by fabric width strips white-on-black floral; subcut strips into two 16½" J strips, four 16½" N strips and four 7½" M strips.

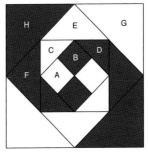

Snail's Trail
7" x 7" Block
Make 22

3. Cut four 1½" by fabric width I strips white-on-black floral.

4. Cut five 3" by fabric width strips black-on-white floral; subcut strips into two 21½" L strips, four 16½" O strips and four 14½" P strips.

5. Cut four 3" by fabric width K strips black-on-white floral.

6. Cut one 8" x 13½" Q zippered-pocket rectangle black-on-white floral.

7. Cut seven 2½" by fabric width strips black-on-white floral for binding. Cut two 22" lengths from strips for pocket binding strips.

Completing the Snail's Trail Blocks

1. To complete one Snail's Trail block, sew an A square to a B square; repeat. Press seams toward B. Join the A-B units to make a Four-Patch unit as shown in Figure 1; press seam to one side.

Figure 1

2. Sew a C triangle to opposite sides of the Four-Patch unit as shown in Figure 2; press seams toward C.

Figure 2   **Figure 3**

3. Sew a D triangle to the remaining sides of the Four-Patch unit to complete the center unit as shown in Figure 3; press seams toward D.

4. Repeat steps 2 and 3 with E and F, and H and G referring to the block drawing for positioning of pieces and pressing pieces toward the most recently added triangles after each addition to complete one Snail's Trail block.

5. Repeat steps 1–4 to complete 22 Snail's Trail blocks.

Completing the Quilt Top

1. Join nine Snail's Trail blocks to make the top row as shown in Figure 4; press seams in one direction. Repeat to make the bottom row, again referring to Figure 4 for positioning of blocks.

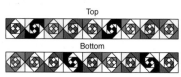

Top

Bottom

Figure 4

2. Join the rows to complete the pieced center referring to the Placement Diagram for positioning; press seam in one direction. *Note: The rows need to be joined in specific positions to create the "trail."*

3. Join I strips on short ends to make one long strip; press seams open. Subcut strip into two 63½" I strips.

4. Sew I strips to opposite long sides and J strips to the short ends of the pieced center; press seams toward I and J strips.

5. Join K strips as in step 3 and subcut into two 65½" K strips.

6. Sew K strips to opposite long sides and L strips to the short ends of the pieced center to complete the pieced top.

7. Sandwich the larger batting rectangle between the completed top and larger prepared backing; pin or baste layers together.

8. Quilt as desired by hand or machine; remove pins or basting. Trim edges even.

9. Set aside and finish pocket units for back side.

Completing the Pocket Units

1. To complete one pocket unit, join two Snail's Trail blocks as shown in Figure 5; press seam to one side.

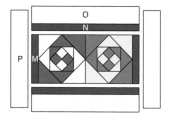

Figure 5

2. Sew M strips to opposite short ends; press seams toward M strips.

3. Sew an N strip to an O strip along length; press seams toward N. Repeat to make two N-O strips.

4. Sew an N-O strip to opposite long sides of the pieced center with O strips on the outside; press seams toward N-O strips.

5. Sew P strip to opposite short ends to complete one pieced pocket unit top.

6. Sandwich a small batting rectangle between the completed top and a small prepared backing; pin or baste layers together.

7. Quilt as desired by hand or machine. When quilting is complete, remove pins or basting. Trim excess backing and batting even with pocket edges.

8. Lay the zipper right side up on a flat surface; center and pin one 8" end of the Q rectangle right side down on the upper edge of the zipper with

Q covering the zipper and raw edges of Q aligned with the edge of the zipper tape.

9. With the zipper side up and using a zipper foot, stitch a generous ¼" seam along the pinned edges as shown in Figure 6; press Q away from zipper. *Note: If you stitch too close to the zipper tab, the zipper won't slide; using a ¼" seam is not enough, but ⅜" is too much.*

Figure 6

10. Repeat steps 8 and 9 with the opposite edge of the zipper to make a zippered tube as shown in Figure 7.

Figure 7

Figure 8

11. Turn the tube wrong side out; open the zipper. Pin raw edges together with zipper 1" down from one end as shown in Figure 8.

12. Stitch along both raw edges to complete the zippered pocket, again referring to Figure 8; trim end of zipper even with fabric edges. Turn right side out through zipper opening.

13. Center and hand-stitch side and bottom edges to the quilted pocket unit, placing top of the zippered pocket 2⅝" from the raw edge of one long side of the pocket unit as shown in Figure 9.

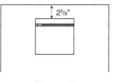

Figure 9

14. From the right side, stitch in the ditch of seam between the N and O pieces to catch the top of the pocket in the stitching.

15. Fold and press a 22" binding strip in half with wrong sides together along length.

16. Matching raw edges, stitch binding to the top zippered-pocket edge of the pocket; turn to the back side and hand- or machine-stitch in place.

17. Repeat steps 1–7 and steps 15 and 16 to complete a second pocket for the opposite end of the shawl.

Completing the Shawl

1. Place a completed pocket right side up on each end of the back side of the quilted top, matching raw edges; machine-baste to hold in place.

2. Join binding strips on short ends with diagonal seams to make one long strip; trim seams to ¼" and press open.

3. Fold binding strip in half with wrong sides together along length; press.

4. Sew binding to the right side of the shawl, mitering corners and overlapping ends; press binding away from edges and turn to the back side. Hand- or machine-stitch in place to finish. ◆

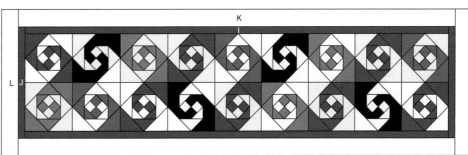

Personality Prayer Shawl
Placement Diagram 70" x 21"

Black & White Plus Red

Change the colors of the English paper-pieced flowers and 16-patch blocks to fit your special occasion.

DESIGN BY CHRIS MALONE

PROJECT SPECIFICATIONS

Skill Level: Intermediate
Quilt Size: 40" x 40"
Block Size: 8" x 8"
Number of Blocks: 9

MATERIALS

- 1 fat quarter orange tonal
- 1 fat quarter red tonal stripe
- 1 fat quarter dark green tonal
- 1 fat quarter lime green tonal
- 2 fat quarters red tonals
- 4 fat quarters black-with-white prints (black)
- 4 fat quarters white-with-black prints (white)
- ⅞ yard black-and-white plaid
- Batting 48" x 48"
- Backing 48" x 48"
- All-purpose thread to match fabrics
- Quilting thread
- 8 (½") black buttons
- 56 precut 1" hexagon paper shapes (optional) or regular-weight white paper
- Water-soluble marker
- Basic sewing tools and supplies

Cutting

1. Cut three 2½" x 21" strips from each of the black and white print fat quarters; subcut strips into (18) 2½" A squares each fabric.

2. Cut nine 2¼" x 21" strips total black and white print fat quarters for binding.

3. Cut two 8½" x 21" strips red tonal stripe; subcut strips into (24) 1½" B strips.

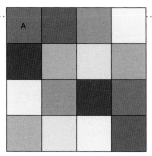

16-Patch
8" x 8" Block
Make 9

4. Cut two 1½" x 21" strips orange tonal; subcut strips into (16) 1½" C squares.

5. Cut two 6½" x 28½" D strips and two 6½" x 40½" E strips black-and-white plaid.

6. Cut eight 1¼" x 15" bias vine strips dark green tonal.

Completing the Blocks

1. Arrange 16 A squares (two of each print) in four rows of four squares each.

2. Join the squares as arranged to make rows; press seams in adjacent rows in opposite directions.

3. Join the rows to complete one 16-Patch block; press seams in one direction.

4. Repeat steps 1–3 to complete nine identical 16-Patch blocks.

Completing the Top

1. Arrange the blocks in three rows of three blocks; join three blocks from one row with four

B strips to make a block row as shown in Figure 1; press seams toward B strips. Repeat to make three block rows.

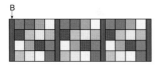
Figure 1

2. Join three B strips with four C squares to make a sashing row as shown in Figure 2; press seams toward B strips. Repeat to make four sashing rows.

Figure 2

3. Join the block rows with the sashing rows to complete the pieced center; press seams toward sashing rows.

4. Sew a D strip to opposite sides and E strips to the top and bottom of the pieced center; press seams toward D and E strips to complete the pieced top.

English Paper Piecing & Appliqué

1. To make the English paper-pieced flowers, copy the hexagon pattern given onto white paper 56 times if not using precut shapes; carefully cut out each shape.

2. Pin the paper hexagon to the wrong side of one of the red tonals; cut the fabric ¼" larger than the paper piece all around as shown in Figure 3. Repeat to cut 24 hexagons from each of the two red tonals and eight from the orange tonal.

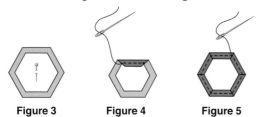
Figure 3   **Figure 4**   **Figure 5**

3. To prepare each hexagon for stitching, fold the ¼" seam allowance over the paper shape at precisely the paper edge; finger-press and hand-baste in place through the fabric and paper using

large stitches as shown in Figure 4. To fold corners, continue to fold over the fabric, but include the folded-over seam allowance from the previous side as shown in Figure 5.

4. Secure basting at the end with a small backstitch; clip thread, leaving a ¼" tail. Repeat to prepare all hexagon shapes for the flowers.

5. To hand-stitch one flower, use six matching red hexagons for the petals and one orange for the center. Place one each orange and red hexagon pieces right sides together, and using a knotted single-strand matching thread, insert the needle at one corner under the seam allowance and out the tip; make small whipstitches to overcast the pieces together, just catching the edges of the fabric and only barely missing the enclosed paper edge. When you have completed the edge, take a second stitch into the corner to secure, and then open the patches flat as shown in Figure 6.

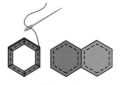
Figure 6   **Figure 7**

6. Place the second red hexagon on top of the first red hexagon with right sides together; whipstitch the edges from the orange center to the outer edge as in step 5. Tie off the thread and clip. Now fold the patches so the second red hexagon is right sides together with the orange center and hand-sew the edges together. Continue around, adding the red petals until the flower is complete as shown in Figure 7; press.

7. Remove the basting stitches; carefully remove the paper pieces.

8. Repeat steps 5–7 to make a total of eight flowers—four from each red tonal.

9. To make vines, fold each dark green bias vine strip in half along length with wrong sides together; stitch a scant ¼" seam along the raw edges. Trim seam to ⅛" and fold the strip so the seam is open and centered down the length of the vine as shown in Figure 8.

Figure 8

10. Using the pattern given and a water-soluble marker, trace 12 leaf shapes and 12 reversed leaf shapes onto the right side of the lime green tonal; cut out shapes, leaving a ⅛"–¼" seam to turn under all around.

11. Turn under edges of each leaf shape along the marked lines, finger-press, and then hand-baste to hold in place.

12. Place a matching flower at each corner and the remaining four flowers centered on each border strip; hand-baste to hold in place.

13. Arrange and pin a vine in a gentle curving line between the flowers, tucking the vine ends at least ¼" under the edge of the flowers; clip any excess.

14. Arrange and pin three leaves on each vine, referring to the Placement Diagram for positioning; hand-stitch flowers, vine and leaf shapes in place using thread to match fabrics to complete the pieced top.

Completing the Quilt

1. Sandwich the batting between the completed top and prepared backing; pin or baste layers together.

2. Quilt as desired by hand or machine. When quilting is complete, trim batting and backing even with edges of the quilted top.

3. Join binding strips on short ends with diagonal seams to make one long strip; trim seams to ¼" and press seams open.

4. Fold binding strip in half wrong sides together along length; press.

5. Sew binding to the right side of the pieced top, matching raw edges, mitering corners and overlapping ends; press binding away from quilt edges and turn to the back side. Hand- or machine-stitch in place.

6. Sew a black button in the center of each hexagon flower to finish. ◆

Black & White Plus Red
Placement Diagram 40" x 40"

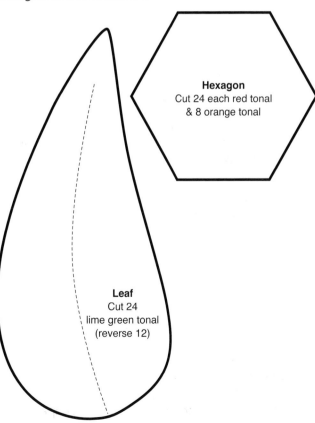

Hexagon
Cut 24 each red tonal
& 8 orange tonal

Leaf
Cut 24
lime green tonal
(reverse 12)

Casablanca

The use of batiks in lights, mediums and darks create a design that is both mysterious and compelling.

DESIGN BY SUSAN KNAPP

PROJECT SPECIFICATIONS

Skill Level: Intermediate
Quilt Size: 44" x 56"
Block Size: 12" x 12"
Number of Blocks: 12

MATERIALS

- 6 fat quarters light-color batiks
- 6 fat quarters medium-color batiks
- 6 fat quarters dark-color batiks
- ⅓ yard cream batik
- ⅝ yard black batik
- Batting 52" x 64"
- Backing 52" x 64"
- All-purpose thread to match fabrics
- Quilting thread
- Basic sewing tools and supplies

Cutting

1. Cut two 3⅞" x 21" strips from each of the light-color fat quarters; subcut strips into eight 3⅞" squares each fabric. Cut each square in half on one diagonal to make 96 A triangles.

2. Cut two 3½" x 21" strips from each of the light-color fat quarters; subcut strips into eight 3½" F squares each fabric.

3. Cut two 3½" x 21" strips from each of the medium- and dark-color fat quarters; set aside one of each strip for M borders. Subcut each of the remaining strips into four 3½" J squares and one 2¾" G square; subcut each remaining dark-color strip into four 3½" I squares and one 2¾" H square.

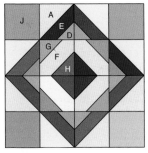

Medium-Corner Casablanca
12" x 12" Block
Make 6

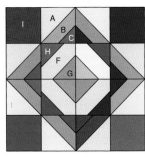

Dark-Corner Casablanca
12" x 12" Block
Make 6

4. Cut one 3⅞" x 21" strip from each of the medium- and dark-color fat quarters; subcut each strip into four 3⅞" squares. Cut each square in half on one diagonal to make 48 each medium B and dark E triangles.

5. Cut one 2¾" x 21" strip from each of the medium- and dark-color fat quarters; subcut each medium-color strip into seven G 2¾" squares and each dark-color strip into seven H 2¾" squares.

6. Cut one 2" x 21" strip from each of the medium- and dark-color fat quarters; subcut each strip into eight 2" D squares, and each dark-color strip into eight 2" C squares.

7. Cut two 1½" x 36½" K strips cream batik.

8. Cut three 1½" by fabric width L strips cream batik.

9. Cut six 2¼" by fabric width strips black batik for binding.

Completing the Blocks

1. Sew a light A to a medium B along the diagonal to make an A-B unit as shown in Figure 1; do not press. Repeat to make 48 A-B units.

Figure 1

2. Draw a diagonal line from corner to corner on the wrong side of each C square.

3. Place a C square right sides together on the B corner of an A-B unit and stitch on the marked line as shown in Figure 2; trim seam to ¼" to complete an A-B-C unit as shown in Figure 3. Repeat to make 48 A-B-C units.

Figure 2 **Figure 3**

4. Press seams on 24 A-B-C units toward A, and on the remaining 24 units toward C as shown in Figure 4.

Make 24 each

Figure 4

5. Repeat steps 1–3 with A, E and D pieces referring to Figure 5; press seams as in step 4 and referring to Figure 6.

Make 24 each

Figure 5 **Figure 6**

6. Draw a diagonal line from corner to corner on the wrong side of each G and H square.

7. Place a G square right sides together on one corner of F; stitch on the marked line as shown in Figure 7; trim seam to ¼". Repeat with H on the opposite corner of F referring to Figure 8 to complete one F-G-H unit. Repeat to make 48 F-G-H units.

Figure 7 **Figure 8**

8. Press seams on 24 F-G-H units toward F, and on the remaining 24 units toward H as shown in Figure 9.

Make 24 each

Figure 9

9. Arrange the stitched units in rows with I, placing the units with seams pressed in the direction of the arrows as shown in Figure 10.

10. Join the units in rows as arranged; pressing seams in the direction of the arrows in each row. Join the rows and press in the direction of the arrows to complete a Dark-Corner Casablanca block, again referring to Figure 10. Repeat to make six blocks.

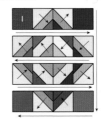 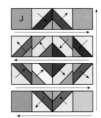

Figure 10 **Figure 11**

11. Repeat steps 9 and 10 with the pieced units and J squares to complete six Medium-Corner Casablanca blocks as shown in Figure 11.

Casablanca
Placement Diagram 44" x 56"

Completing the Top

1. Join two Medium-Corner Casablanca blocks with one Dark-Corner Casablanca block to make an X row as shown in Figure 12; press seams in one direction. Repeat to make two X rows.

2. Join two Dark-Corner Casablanca blocks with one Medium-Corner Casablanca block to make a Y row, again referring to Figure 12; press seams in one direction. Repeat to make two Y rows.

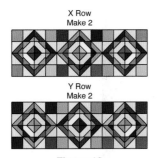

X Row
Make 2

Y Row
Make 2

Figure 12

3. Alternate and join rows with seams in adjoining rows pressed in opposite directions to complete the pieced center; press seams in one direction.

4. Sew a K strip to the top and bottom of the pieced center; press seams toward K strips.

5. Join the L strips on short ends to make one long strip; press seams open. Subcut strip into two 50½" L strips.

6. Sew L strips to opposite long sides of the pieced center; press seams toward L strips.

7. Trim the M border strips to 17½"; determine placement around edges and join on the short ends in sets of three to make four M strips.

8. Fold each M strip in half along length and crease to mark the center; repeat with the pieced center.

9. Matching the creases, sew an M strip to opposite sides of the pieced center; trim excess at each end even with the pieced center and press seams toward M strips.

10. Repeat step 9 with M strips on the top and bottom of the pieced center to complete the pieced top.

Completing the Quilt

1. Sandwich the batting between the completed top and prepared backing; pin or baste layers together.

2. Quilt as desired by hand or machine. When quilting is complete, trim batting and backing even with edges of the quilted top.

3. Join binding strips on short ends with diagonal seams to make one long strip; trim seams to ¼" and press seams open.

4. Fold binding strip in half wrong sides together along length; press.

5. Sew binding to the right side of the pieced top, matching raw edges, mitering corners and overlapping ends; press binding away from quilt edges and turn to the back side. Hand- or machine-stitch in place. ◆

Starry Night

Two traditional quilt blocks, Pinwheel Star and Churn Dash, combine to create a star-studded quilt design.

DESIGN BY JILL REBER

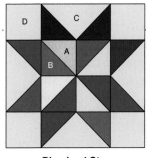

Pinwheel Star
10" x 10" Block
Make 18

Churn Dash
10" x 10" Block
Make 17

PROJECT SPECIFICATIONS

Skill Level: Beginner
Quilt Size: 60" x 80"
Block Size: 10" x 10"
Number of Blocks: 35

MATERIALS

- 9 different fat quarters dark blue
- 9 different fat quarters yellow
- 1¼ yards navy print
- 2 yards light blue print
- Batting 68" x 88"
- Backing 68" x 88"
- All-purpose thread to match fabrics
- Quilting thread
- Basic sewing tools and supplies

Cutting

1. Cut one 5½" x 21" strip from each of the nine dark blue fat quarters; subcut each strip into two 5½" F squares. Set aside one F square for another use.

2. Cut two 3⅜" x 21" strips from each of the nine dark blue fat quarters; subcut strips to make a total of (108) 3⅜" squares. Cut each square in half on one diagonal to make 216 B triangles.

3. Cut two 3⅜" x 21" strips from each of the nine yellow fat quarters; subcut strips to make a total of (70) 3⅜" squares. Cut each square in half on one diagonal to make 140 A triangles.

4. Cut one 5½" x 21" strip from each of the nine yellow fat quarters; subcut strips to make a total of (68) 1¾" G rectangles.

5. Cut two 2½" x 21" binding strips from each of the nine yellow fat quarters.

6. Cut six 3" by fabric width strips light blue print; subcut strips into (72) 3" D squares.

7. Cut three 6¼" by fabric width strips light blue print; subcut strips into (18) 6¼" squares. Cut each square on both diagonals to make 72 C triangles.

8. Cut three 5½" by fabric width strips light blue print; subcut strips into (68) 1¾" H rectangles.

9. Cut three 3⅜" by fabric width strips light blue print; subcut strips into (34) 3⅜" squares. Cut each square in half on one diagonal to make 68 E triangles.

10. Cut seven 5½" by fabric width I/J strips navy print.

Completing the Pinwheel Star Blocks

1. Sew an A triangle to a B triangle along the diagonal to make an A-B unit as shown in Figure 1; press seam toward B. Repeat to make 72 A-B units.

Figure 1

2. Sew a B triangle to each short side of C to make a B-C unit as shown in Figure 2; press seams toward B. Repeat to make 72 B-C units.

Figure 2   **Figure 3**

3. To complete one Pinwheel Star block, join two A-B units to make a row as shown in Figure 3; press seam toward the darker side. Repeat to make a second row. Join the two rows to complete the center pinwheel unit; press seam to one side.

4. Sew a B-C unit to opposite sides of the center pinwheel unit to complete the center row as shown in Figure 4; press seams toward the center pinwheel unit.

Figure 4   **Figure 5**

5. Sew a D square to each end of a B-C unit to make a B-C-D row referring to Figure 5; press seams toward D. Repeat to make two B-C-D rows.

6. Sew a B-C-D row to the top and bottom of the center row to complete one Pinwheel Star block referring to the block drawing; press seams away from the center row.

7. Repeat steps 3–6 to complete 18 Pinwheel Star blocks.

Completing the Churn Dash Blocks

1. Sew G to H along the 5½" side as shown in Figure 6; press seam toward H. Repeat to make 68 G-H units.

Figure 6   **Figure 7**

2. Sew A to E along the diagonal to make an A-E unit as shown in Figure 7; press seams toward E. Repeat to make 68 A-E units.

3. To complete one Churn Dash block, sew a G-H unit to opposite sides of F to make the center row as shown in Figure 8; press seams toward the G-H units.

Figure 8   **Figure 9**

4. Sew an A-E unit to each end of a G-H unit to make the top row as shown in Figure 9; press seams toward the G-H unit. Repeat to make the bottom row.

5. Sew the top and bottom rows to the center row referring to the block drawing to complete the Churn Dash block; press seams toward the center row.

6. Repeat steps 3–5 to complete 17 Churn Dash blocks.

Starry Night
Placement Diagram 60" x 80"

Completing the Top

1. Arrange and join two Churn Dash blocks with three Pinwheel Star blocks to make an X row as shown in Figure 10; press seams toward Churn Dash blocks. Repeat to make four X rows.

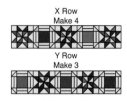

X Row
Make 4

Y Row
Make 3

Figure 10

2. Arrange and join two Pinwheel Star blocks with three Churn Dash blocks to make a Y row, again referring to Figure 10; press seams toward Churn Dash blocks. Repeat to make three Y rows.

3. Join the X and Y rows, beginning and ending with an X row to complete the pieced center; press seams in one direction.

4. Join the I/J strips on short ends to make one long strip; press seams open. Subcut strip into two 70½" I strips and two 60½" J strips.

5. Sew the I strips to opposite long sides and J strips to the top and bottom of the pieced center; press seams toward I and J strips to complete the pieced top.

Completing the Quilt

1. Sandwich the batting between the completed top and prepared backing; pin or baste layers together.

2. Quilt as desired by hand or machine. When quilting is complete, trim batting and backing even with edges of the quilted top.

3. Join binding strips on short ends with diagonal seams to make one long strip; trim seams to ¼" and press seams open.

4. Fold binding strip in half wrong sides together along length; press.

5. Sew binding to the right side of the top, matching raw edges, mitering corners and overlapping ends; press binding away from quilt edges and turn to the back side. Hand- or machine-stitch in place to finish. ◆

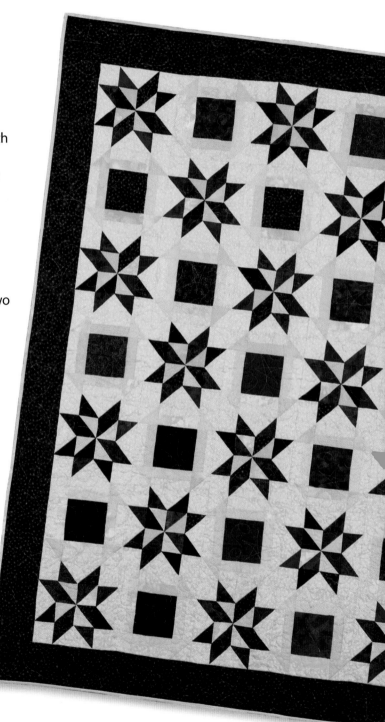

Snowballs in Plaids

This design can be made with scraps as easily as with fat quarters since each 12 x 12-inch block uses only two fabrics—one light and one dark.

DESIGN BY JULIA DUNN

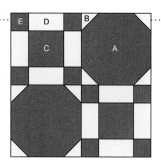

Snowball & Nine-Patch
12" x 12" Block
Make 25

PROJECT NOTE

The designer mixed fat quarters and scraps to make this quilt. These instructions are written to use only fat quarters.

PROJECT SPECIFICATIONS

Skill Level: Beginner
Quilt Size: 68" x 68"
Block Size: 12" x 12"
Number of Blocks: 25

MATERIALS

- 25 fat quarters plaids or homespuns
- 25 fat quarters cream/tan solids or tonals
- ¼ yard burgundy solid
- ½ yard cream tonal
- 1⅛ yards burgundy plaid
- Batting 76" x 76"
- Backing 76" x 76"
- All-purpose thread to match fabrics
- Quilting thread
- Basic sewing tools and supplies

Cutting

1. From each plaid or homespun fat quarter, cut two 6½" x 6½" A squares, two 3½" x 3½" C squares and eight 2" x 2" E squares. Pin same-fabric pieces together to make a block set. You will need 25 block sets.

2. From each cream/tan fat quarter, cut eight 2" x 2" B squares and eight 2" x 3½" D rectangles.

Pin same-fabric pieces together to make a block set. You will need 25 block sets.

3. Cut six 1" by fabric width F/G strips burgundy solid.

4. Cut seven 2" by fabric width H/I strips cream tonal.

5. Cut seven 2½" by fabric width J/K strips burgundy plaid.

6. Cut seven 2¼" by fabric width binding strips burgundy plaid.

Completing the Blocks

1. To complete one Snowball & Nine-Patch block, select one set of cream/tan pieces and one set of plaid/homespun pieces.

2. Draw a diagonal line from corner to corner on the wrong side of each B square.

3. Pin a B square right sides together on each corner of A as shown in Figure 1.

Figure 1

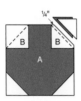
4. Referring to Figure 2, stitch on the marked lines, trim seam to ¼" and press B to the right side on each corner to complete one snowball unit. Repeat to make a second matching snowball unit.

Figure 2   Figure 3

5. Sew D to opposite sides of C to make a C-D unit as shown in Figure 3; press seams toward C.

6. Sew E to each end of each remaining D rectangle to make two D-E units as shown in Figure 4; press seams toward E.

Figure 4

7. Sew a D-E unit to opposite sides of the C-D unit to complete one Nine-Patch unit. Repeat to make a matching Nine-Patch unit.

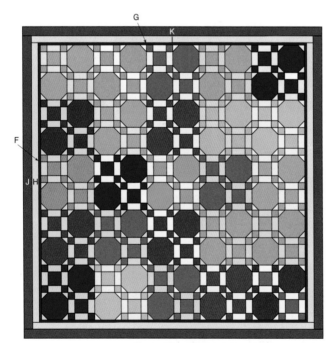

Snowballs in Plaid
Placement Diagram 68" x 68"

8. Join one each Snowball and Nine-Patch unit to make a row; press seam toward the Nine-Patch unit. Repeat to make two rows.

9. Join the rows referring to the block drawing to complete one Snowball & Nine-Patch block; press seam in one direction.

10. Repeat steps 1–9 to complete 25 Snowball & Nine-Patch blocks.

Completing the Top

1. Arrange and join five Snowball & Nine-Patch blocks to make a row; press seams in one direction. Repeat to make five rows.

2. Join the rows referring to the Placement Diagram for positioning; press seams in one direction to complete the pieced center.

3. Join the F/G strips on short ends to make one long strip; press seams open. Subcut strip into two 60½" F strips and two 61½" G strips.

4. Sew the F strips to opposite sides and G strips to the top and bottom of the pieced center; press seams toward F and G strips.

5. Join the H/I strips on short ends to make one long strip; press seams open. Subcut strip into two 61½" H strips and two 64½" I strips.

6. Sew an H strip to opposite long sides and I strips to the top and bottom of the pieced center; press seams toward H and I strips.

7. Join the J/K strips on short ends to make one long strip; press seams open. Subcut strip into two 64½" J strips and two 68½" K strips.

8. Sew a J strip to opposite long sides and K strips to the top and bottom of the pieced center; press seams toward J and K strips to complete the pieced top.

Completing the Quilt

1. Sandwich the batting between the completed top and prepared backing; pin or baste layers together.

2. Quilt as desired by hand or machine. When quilting is complete, trim batting and backing even with edges of the quilted top.

3. Join binding strips on short ends with diagonal seams to make one long strip; trim seams to ¼" and press seams open.

4. Fold binding strip in half wrong sides together along length; press.

5. Sew binding to the right side of the top, matching raw edges, mitering corners and overlapping ends; press binding away from quilt edges and turn to the back side. Hand- or machine-stitch in place to finish. ◆

Summer Fixin's

Continued from page 117

2. Join the rows, turning every other row to offset pieces referring to the Placement Diagram for positioning; press seams in one direction to complete the pieced center.

3. Join the E strips on short ends to make one long strip; press seams open. Subcut strip into two 50" E strips.

4. Sew the E strips to opposite long sides and F strips to the top and bottom of the pieced center; press seams toward E and F strips.

5. Join the G/H strips on short ends to make one long strip; press seams open. Subcut strip into two 54" G strips and two 52" H strips.

6. Sew the G strips to opposite long sides and H strips to the top and bottom of the pieced center; press seams toward G and H strips to complete the pieced top.

Completing the Quilt

1. Sandwich the batting between the completed top and prepared backing; pin or baste layers together.

2. Quilt as desired by hand or machine. When quilting is complete, trim batting and backing even with edges of the quilted top.

3. Join binding strips on short ends with diagonal seams to make one long strip; trim seams to ¼" and press seams open.

4. Fold binding strip in half wrong sides together along length; press.

5. Sew binding to the right side of the quilted top, matching raw edges, mitering corners and overlapping ends; press binding away from quilt edges and turn to the back side. Hand- or machine-stitch in place to finish. ◆

Warm Breeze Runner

Continued from page 96

6. Sew the end units to each I end of the pieced center referring to the Placement Diagram for positioning; press seams toward I.

7. Sew an M strip to opposite short ends of the pieced center; press seams toward M strips.

8. Join the N strips on short ends to make one long strip; press seams open. Subcut strip into two 60" N strips.

9. Sew an N strip to opposite long sides of the pieced center; press seams toward N strips to complete the pieced top.

10. Sandwich batting between the pieced top and prepared backing; pin or baste layers together.

11. Quilt as desired by hand or machine. When quilting is complete, remove pins or basting and trim excess backing and batting even with runner edges.

12. Join binding strips on short ends to make one long strip; press seams open. Fold strip with wrong sides together along length; press.

13. Sew binding to the right side of the runner with raw edges even, mitering corners and overlapping ends; press binding away from runner edges and turn to the back side. Hand- or machine-stitch in place to finish. ◆

Zoo-Friendly Packs

Continued from page 134

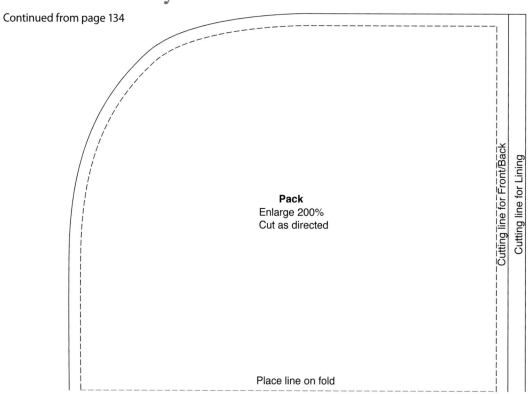

Pack
Enlarge 200%
Cut as directed

Cutting line for Front/Back

Cutting line for Lining

Place line on fold

Sewing Room Boutique

Continued from page 143

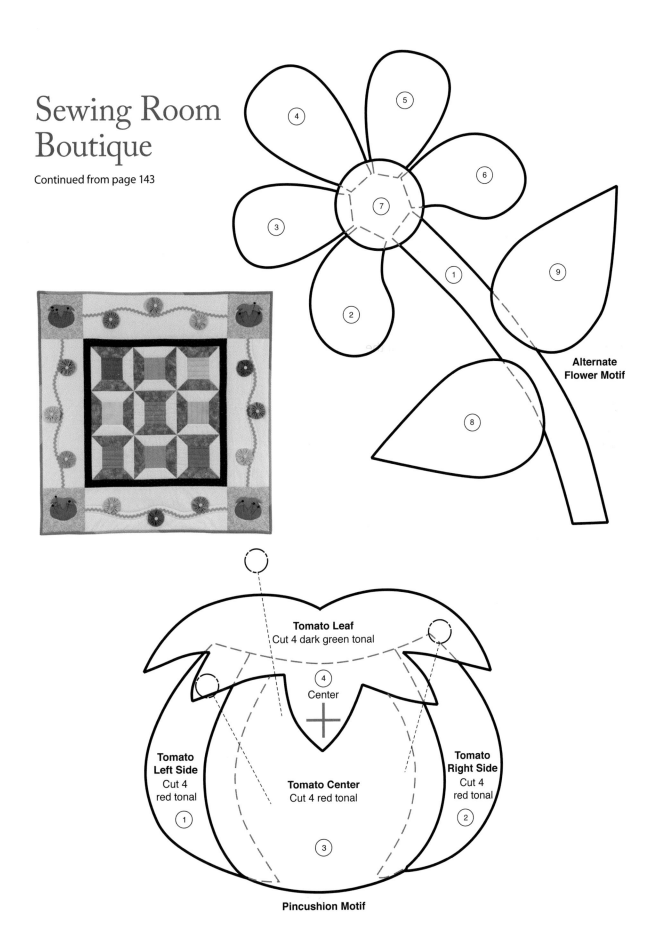

④
⑤
④
⑥
③
⑦
①
②
⑨

Alternate Flower Motif

⑧

Tomato Leaf
Cut 4 dark green tonal

④
Center

Tomato Left Side
Cut 4 red tonal
①

Tomato Center
Cut 4 red tonal
③

Tomato Right Side
Cut 4 red tonal
②

Pincushion Motif

Oriental Lanterns

Continued from page 149

4. Sew a C strip to a D strip along length to make a C-D strip set; press seam toward D. Repeat to make three C-D strip sets.

5. Subcut the C-D strip sets into (24) 4½" C-D units as shown in Figure 3.

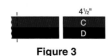

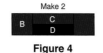

Figure 3   **Figure 4**

6. To complete one Oriental Lantern block, sew a B square to each end of two C-D units to make two rows as shown in Figure 4; press seams toward C-D.

7. Sew a row to the top and bottom of an A-B unit; press seams toward the rows to complete one block.

8. Repeat steps 6 and 7 to complete 12 Oriental Lantern blocks.

Completing the Top

1. Join four Oriental Lantern blocks to make a vertical row; press seams in one direction. Repeat to make three rows.

2. Join the rows with E strips, beginning and ending with an E strip; press seams toward E strips.

3. Sew an F strip to the top and bottom of the pieced center; press seams toward F strips.

4. Join the G strips on short ends to make one long strip; press seams open. Subcut strip into two 44½" G strips.

5. Sew a G strip to opposite long sides and H strips to the top and bottom of the pieced center; press seams toward G and H strips to complete the pieced top.

Completing the Quilt

1. Sandwich the batting between the completed top and prepared backing piece; pin or baste layers together.

2. Quilt as desired by hand or machine. When quilting is complete, trim batting and backing even with edges of the quilted top.

3. Machine-stitch a curving handle line, using gold metallic thread, from corner to corner of the C pieces at the top of each block.

4. Join binding strips on short ends with diagonal seams to make one long strip; trim seams to ¼" and press seams open.

5. Fold binding strip in half wrong sides together along length; press.

6. Sew binding to the right side of the pieced top, matching raw edges, mitering corners and overlapping ends; press binding away from quilt edges and turn to the back side. Hand- or machine-stitch in place to finish. ◆

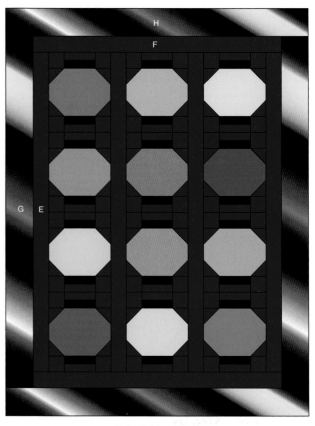

Oriental Lanterns
Placement Diagram 40" x 52"

Fabric & Supplies

Page 6: Holly Tree Skirt—Bosal fusible web and fusible fleece batting and Microtex 70/10 needle.

Page 11: Flower-Fresh Magnet Message Board—Message board from The Wood Connection.

Page 25: Reversible Walker Bag—Fabric from Exclusively Quilters and Dual Duty XP thread from Coats.

Page 28: Fish Pocket Purse—Viking specialty feet.

Page 36: The Maze Table Runner—Warm & Natural cotton batting from The Warm Company.

Page 49: Autumn Place Mats—Insul-bright batting from The Warm Company and fabric from Princess Mirah Bali Fabrics.

Page 52: Petal Pillow—Rose Cuddle microfleece from Shannon Fabrics Inc.

Page 55: Chicks Pocket Pillow—Wynken, Blynken & Nod fabric collection from Quilting Treasures by Cranston Print Works.

Page 58: One, Two, Three Little Chickens—Steam-A-Seam fusible web from The Warm Company and Fabri-Tac permanent fabric adhesive.

Page 62: "Life of the Party" Dog Coat—It's a Dog's Life fabric collection by Phyllis Dobbs for Quilting Treasures, Warm & Natural cotton batting and Steam-A-Seam 2 fusible web from The Warm Company, Blendables multicolored cotton thread from Sulky of America and Dual XP all-purpose thread from Coats.

Page 84: Cone Flower Wall Hanging—Bosal fusible web and Princess Mirah Bali Fabrics batiks.

Page 90: Big Bead Bag--ShirTailor 22"-wide lightweight fusible interfacing from Pellon.

Page 97: Americana Checkerboard—Checker discs from Casey's Wood Products. (800) 452-2739 or www.caseyswood.com.

Page 102: Bags in Blue—Bosal fusible batting.

Page 117: Summer Fixin's—Farmer's Market fabrics from RJR Fabrics and Warm & Natural batting from The Warm Company.

Page 123: 21-Strip Salute—Spice Market fabric collection from Exclusively Quilters.

Page 131: Zoo-Friendly Packs—Steam-A-Seam 2 fusible web from The Warm Company.

Page 136: Winter Friends—Lite Steam-A-Seam 2 and Warm & Natural cotton batting from The Warm Company.

Page 154: Black & White Plus Red—Paper Pieces at (800) 337-1537 or www.paperpieces.com.

Page 163: Starry Night—Master Piece 45 ruler and Static Stickers from Master Piece Products.

Special Thanks

Please join us in thanking the talented designers below.

Photo Index

90 Big Bead Bag

94 Warm Breeze Runner

97 Americana Checkerboard

102 Bags in Blue

106 Fun-to-Cook Apron

109 Easy Praire Runner

112 Christmas Square Tree Skirt

117 Summer Fixin's

118 Cherry Pickin'

123 21-Strip Salute

126 Reversible Flower Pillow

131 Zoo-Friendly Packs

136 Winter Friends

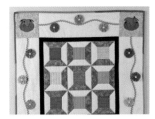

140 Sewing Room Boutique

145 Floating Gems

149 Oriental Lanterns

151 Personality Prayer Shawl

154 Black & White Plus Red

158 Casablanca

163 Starry Night

166 Snowballs in Plaids

Finishing Instructions

When you have completed the quilt top as instructed with patterns, finish your quilt with these four easy steps.

1. Sandwich the batting between the completed top and prepared backing; pin or baste layers together to hold. ***Note:*** *If using basting spray to hold layers together, refer to instructions on the product container for use.*

2. Quilt as desired by hand or machine; remove pins or basting. Trim excess backing and batting even with quilt top.

3. Join binding strips on short ends to make one long strip. Fold the strip in half along length with wrong sides together; press.

4. Sew binding to quilt edges, mitering corners and overlapping ends. Fold binding to the back side and stitch in place to finish. ◆

Metric Conversion Charts

Metric Conversions

Canada/U.S. Measurement		Multiplied by		Metric Measurement
yards	x	.9144	=	metres (m)
yards	x	91.44	=	centimetres (cm)
inches	x	2.54	=	centimetres (cm)
inches	x	25.40	=	millimetres (mm)
inches	x	.0254	=	metres (m)

Canada/U.S. Measurement		Multiplied by		Metric Measurement
centimetres	x	.3937	=	inches
metres	x	1.0936	=	yards

Standard Equivalents

Canada/U.S. Measurement		Metric Measurement		
⅛ inch	=	3.20 mm	=	0.32 cm
¼ inch	=	6.35 mm	=	0.635 cm
⅜ inch	=	9.50 mm	=	0.95 cm
½ inch	=	12.70 mm	=	1.27 cm
⅝ inch	=	15.90 mm	=	1.59 cm
¾ inch	=	19.10 mm	=	1.91 cm
⅞ inch	=	22.20 mm	=	2.22 cm
1 inch	=	25.40 mm	=	2.54 cm
⅛ yard	=	11.43 cm	=	0.11 m
¼ yard	=	22.86 cm	=	0.23 m
⅜ yard	=	34.29 cm	=	0.34 m
½ yard	=	45.72 cm	=	0.46 m
⅝ yard	=	57.15 cm	=	0.57 m
¾ yard	=	68.58 cm	=	0.69 m
⅞ yard	=	80.00 cm	=	0.80 m
1 yard	=	91.44 cm	=	0.91 m
1⅛ yards	=	102.87 cm	=	1.03 m
1¼ yards	=	114.30 cm	=	1.14 m

Canada/U.S. Measurement				Metric Measurement
1⅜ yards	=	125.73 cm	=	1.26 m
1½ yards	=	137.16 cm	=	1.37 m
1⅝ yards	=	148.59 cm	=	1.49 m
1¾ yards	=	160.02 cm	=	1.60 m
1⅞ yards	=	171.44 cm	=	1.71 m
2 yards	=	182.88 cm	=	1.83 m
2⅛ yards	=	194.31 cm	=	1.94 m
2¼ yards	=	205.74 cm	=	2.06 m
2⅜ yards	=	217.17 cm	=	2.17 m
2½ yards	=	228.60 cm	=	2.29 m
2⅝ yards	=	240.03 cm	=	2.40 m
2¾ yards	=	251.46 cm	=	2.51 m
2⅞ yards	=	262.88 cm	=	2.63 m
3 yards	=	274.32 cm	=	2.74 m
3⅛ yards	=	285.75 cm	=	2.86 m
3¼ yards	=	297.18 cm	=	2.97 m
3⅜ yards	=	308.61 cm	=	3.09 m
3½ yards	=	320.04 cm	=	3.20 m
3⅝ yards	=	331.47 cm	=	3.31 m
3¾ yards	=	342.90 cm	=	3.43 m
3⅞ yards	=	354.32 cm	=	3.54 m
4 yards	=	365.76 cm	=	3.66 m
4⅛ yards	=	377.19 cm	=	3.77 m
4¼ yards	=	388.62 cm	=	3.89 m
4⅜ yards	=	400.05 cm	=	4.00 m
4½ yards	=	411.48 cm	=	4.11 m
4⅝ yards	=	422.91 cm	=	4.23 m
4¾ yards	=	434.34 cm	=	4.34 m
4⅞ yards	=	445.76 cm	=	4.46 m
5 yards	=	457.20 cm	=	4.57 m